Advancing . . . # The Smaller Church

by
W. Curry
Mavis,
M.Th., Ph.D.

Baker Book House
Grand Rapids, Michigan

ISBN: 0-8010-5886-4

Reprinted by
Baker Book House Company

First printing, February 1968
Second printing, January 1969
Third printing, September 1971

To My Wife

Marion De Mund Mavis

Foreword

Smaller local churches can succeed. Some of them are thriving now under the blessing of God. These thriving churches have a healthy sense of well being, a clear vision of their task, a compelling sense of mission, and an effective outreach into their communities. Many other smaller congregations should become more effective.

Size is significant in determining the character of churches. Smaller congregations have many of the marked limitations and the stubborn problems that inhere generally in small social groups. On the other hand, they have certain advantages and resources in the close personal relationships between pastor and members, the meaningful personal interaction of their people and, as found in many little congregations, a serious concern about spiritual matters.

This book is concerned with basic principles that underlie effective work in smaller churches. It assumes that these churches must meet a twofold condition for success. First, they must face realistically their problems and, secondly, they must capitalize upon their resources.

The materials in this volume are concerned with smaller congregations in both urban and rural situations. There are thousands of smaller churches in our cities as well as in rural areas. All of these churches have some of the problems that are inherent in smaller groups.

There is little contemporary literature on the unique religious, psychological, and sociological problems of smaller congregations. There are many fine books, of course, that deal specifically with the problems of rural churches. Little congregations, even those in rural settings, however, have problems that are not inherently related to a rural situation.

This book is written for all who are concerned about

smaller churches. It is hoped that ministers will get new insights into ways of advancing the Kingdom of God as they read its pages. We trust also that laymen will find this material illuminating and helpful.

W. Curry Mavis

Contents

1. THE SIGNIFICANCE OF SMALLER CHURCHES   9
   Defining the Smaller Church
   Historical Significance of Smaller Religious Groups
   Contemporary Significance of Smaller Churches

2. THE GENIUS OF SMALLER CHURCHES - - 21
   Spiritual Growth Through Fellowship
   Spiritual Growth Through Personal Participation
   Spiritual Growth Through Christian Service

3. THE TENDENCY TOWARD INTROVERSION - 30
   The Struggle for Survival
   Pampering the Saints
   Spiritual Hospitality

4. MAINTAINING MORALE - - - - - - 42
   The Importance of Morale
   The Problem of Status
   Avoiding Personality Tensions
   Getting a Sense of Achievement

5. PLANNING FOR ACTION - - - - - - 54
   Appraising Resources
   Surveying Community Needs and Opportunities
   Setting Goals

6. TRAINING THE WORKERS - - - - - - 66
   A New Day for Laymen
   Enlisting Workers
   Training Workers

7. ORGANIZING FOR ACTION - - - - - - 78
   Setting Up an Organization
   Planning the Work of a Circuit
   Supervising the Work

8. CARRYING ON A COMPREHENSIVE PROGRAM   91

    Defining the Christian Pattern
    Demonstrating the Gospel

9. MAKING ENDS MEET - - - - - - - 105

    Educating for Stewardship
    Raising the Budget
    Providing Adequate Plant and Facilities

10. PERSONALIZING PUBLICITY - - - - - 117

    Person-to-Person Publicity
    Using the Mailing List
    Getting in the Newspapers
    Using Permanent Advertisements

11. CARING FOR THE FLOCK - - - - - - 129

    Defining the Pastoral Personality
    Organizing Pastoral Work

12. WORSHIPING IN THE SMALLER CHURCH - - 142

    Securing Proper Conditions for Worship
    Singing in Smaller Congregations
    The Primacy of Preaching

13. ADVANCING THROUGH CHRISTIAN EDUCA-
    TION - - - - - - - - - - - - - 157

    Outreach Through Christian Education
    Conserving the Results

14. ADVANCING THROUGH EVANGELISM - - 168

    Advancing Through Lay Witnessing
    Advancing Through Revivals

The Significance of Smaller Churches

1

Are smaller local churches the poor relations of larger congregations? Must larger congregations in denominations apologize for the little groups? In community relationships, must the little churches be highly self-conscious about their size? Must Christians belonging to smaller local churches reluctantly acknowledge, "I belong to the little church down the street?"

There are leaders in American Protestantism who answer these questions in the affirmative. They believe that the work of God is hindered greatly by the multiplicity of local churches. They think that Protestantism would gain if many of the smaller churches were closed. I recently heard a learned professor, cloistered in the security of a great divinity school, plead for a movement that would merge all congregations with fewer than 300 members.

We take a different position in this book. We hold that smaller churches are uniquely important and that they have an invaluable genius. We recognize, of course, that there are local churches that are not needed in their communities and where this situation prevails these churches ought to be merged with others. On the other hand, there are thousands of small churches that God needs greatly and these groups must be strengthened.

Defining the Smaller Church

Churches with Sunday morning congregations and Sunday

schools of fewer than 150 may be considered as smaller. This definition views church size on the basis of the number of participants rather than on the basis of a static church membership roll, perhaps long overdue for revision. A functional definition of church size is necessary also because churches differ greatly on their standards of membership.

Recent public opinion polls have indicated that from one-third to one-half of the members in Protestant churches in America may be found in morning worship services on any given Sunday. That suggests the average local church with a worship congregation of 150 has a membership roll of more than three hundred names.

We recognize that there are local churches that are exceptions to this norm, especially in some of the smaller denominations. Some local churches maintain membership rolls on the basis of active Christians and a great number of them have worship congregations and Sunday schools that exceed by far the number of their members.

Our definition of the smaller church, it would appear, includes about one-half of the 273,000 Protestant local churches in the United States. On the basis of the membership rolls, American Protestant churches actually average only about 210 members each.[1] The Sunday schools average an enrollment of about 145.[2] In both worship services and Sunday schools, as suggested above, the actual attendance is much below the membership lists in most cases.

Most of the smaller churches, whether tiny or larger, carry on their work in a social-psychological atmosphere that is characterized by limitations. First, there is usually a lack of denominational and community status. It is sometimes assumed that little churches are failing churches. Denominational leaders often do not see the opportunities of the smaller groups.

---

[1] Landis Y. Benson, *Yearbook of American Churches for 1956* (New York: National Council of Churches of Christ, 1955), p. 237.
[2] *Ibid.*, p. 249.

The lack of status occasions morale problems, and vision and enthusiasm are diminished. Secondly, there is frequently a lack of workers. Sometimes there is only part-time pastoral service and that is on a short-tenure basis. At best, few smaller churches can have any paid personnel other than the minister. Even though he spends all of his time at one church this means that he must often do his own secretarial work and attend to many little tasks from which the preacher in a large congregation is free. Much of the church work is done by laymen in the smaller groups and there is often a shortage of these workers. Frequently important work remains undone because there is no one to whom it may be assigned. Thirdly, there is usually limited finance in smaller churches. This limitation also has wide ramifications. The pastor's salary is usually below the level that would enable him to serve at his best. Lack of funds also means that plant and facilities are not what they should be for maximum effectiveness. These three outstanding limitations, and sometimes others, tend to produce a social-psychological atmosphere characterized by discouragement and frustration.

There are a number of reasons why churches are smaller. In the first place, some are small because of the sparse populations of their communities. This means, quite naturally, a limited numerical potential. Had Robinson Crusoe been properly ordained and appointed to his desert island, he would have found it impossible to raise up a flourishing congregation. Secondly, sometimes churches ministering to racial groups are small because they, too, have a limited potential of numbers, though located in great urban centers. Thirdly, there are churches that are small because of narrow and highly sectarian emphases. Their programs, lacking the breadth of the gospel, appeal to few people. Fourthly, some churches are small because they are actually in an "overchurched" community. Where this situation really prevails, churches that are not needed should be merged with others. Fifth, there are churches that are small, particularly in the number of their adherents, because of the high standards they maintain for membership. These churches frequently have many people participating in their programs who are not actually members. Sixth, there are other churches that are small because they are new and they have not had time to grow. Finally, a great many churches are little because they have not met their problems realistically nor organized an effective plan of outreach. The greatest number of smaller churches are in this class. This book has a special interest in them.

Historical Significance of Smaller Religious Groups

Before the rise of the Christian church the Jewish synagogue had demonstrated the value of smaller religious groups. The synagogue had an informal service consisting of the study of the Law and prayer that was ideally suited to small groups. Synagogues were often organized with little companies of people because only ten men were needed as charter members and services might be held if ten persons were present. Synagogues throughout the Roman Empire in the pre-Christian centuries were often small because of the limited number of Jews living in the towns and smaller cities. Moreover, there was a strong impulse to keep the synagogues small even in areas where there were large numbers of Jews. One tradition states that there were 394 synagogues in Jerusalem shortly before its destruction in 70 A.D. Another tradition puts the figure at 480. Even with a reduction in the number of synagogues suggested above and with a generous estimate of Jerusalem's population at that time, it would seem that there was a synagogue for every 100 adults of Jerusalem's population.

The synagogues, as small religious organizations devoted to the personal instruction and care of the people, did much to perpetuate the Jewish faith. They were far more significant along this line than was the temple during the days of its existence. From the present perspective, it appears that both the Jewish faith and race would have become extinct had it not been for these small groups of religious people that strength-ened each other by instruction, worship, and fellowship.

In laying the foundation for his Kingdom, Jesus chose to work intimately with a small group of men. He spoke, indeed, to the multitudes but those persons who really caught his spirit had a personal relationship with him. Jesus knew that he could accomplish more with twelve men who were thoroughly com-mitted to him than with a multitude who gave only casual assent to his message.

The Christian church itself took root in small groups of believers thoroughly dedicated to Christ. The earliest Chris-tians met, for most part, in the homes of believers and soon these homes came to be known as "house churches." Fre-quently the owners of the homes were the leaders of the Christian groups as in the case of Aquila and Priscilla (Ro-mans 16:3-5). The house churches became numerous even in the Apostolic age. A few of them are mentioned by Paul (1 Corinthians 16:15; Colossians 4:15; Philemon 2; Romans 16:4). Thomas Lindsay believes there were five house churches in Rome at the time Paul wrote his Epistle to the Christians there.[8]

The house churches were commonly used by the Christians during the first generations of our faith. These places con-tinued until the beginning of the third century excepting, per-haps, in a few of the larger towns. Special buildings for wor-ship did not appear until the close of the second century at which time hall churches were designed to accommodate the larger crowds.

The Christian movement gained its strength for its con-quest of the Roman Empire when it was nurtured in small groups of Christians meeting in the homes of believers. In those small groups the believers strengthened each other by

[8] T. M. Lindsay, The Church and the Ministry in the Early Centuries (Lon-don: Hodder and Stoughton, 1903), p. 42.

their fellowship. They studied together the great truths of their faith. They inspired each other for witnessing as they talked together about what God had done for them.

Reforming movements within the Christian church have been nurtured and sustained in small groups of earnest Christians. Little bands of Waldenses recovered some of the central truths of Apostolic Christianity in the twelfth and thirteenth centuries and they bore an effective witness to those truths in Northern Italy. At about the same time, Francis of Assisi and his fellow "imitators of Christ" vividly demonstrated certain Christian virtues and preached clearly gospel truths to the people of Italy and Central Europe. This resulted in the most virile reform of Medieval Christianity. Later, the Lollards in England, small groups of lay preachers and earnest Christians under the leadership of John Wycliffe, called for a return to Apostolic simplicity and sincerity. The Hussites in Bohemia contributed tremendously to a ground swell of evangelical convictions that gave rise to the Protestant Reformation. The Quakers in seventeenth century England protested empty and compromised practices of contemporary Christianity. They were persecuted rigorously, like most reformers, but they were sustained by the fellowship of likeminded believers in their little meetings.

The great Evangelical revival of the eighteenth century was born in small religious groups. The leaders of the revival, John and Charles Wesley and George Whitefield, were members of a Holy Club in Oxford. It should be recognized, however, that a preparation for a spiritual awakening had been going on for many years in small groups both within and without the established church. For two generations devout people of the Church of England had met in small religious societies, much like contemporary prayer groups, for the promotion of "real holiness of heart and life." Many of the dissenting groups, all small in number, had laid an emphasis upon the purity of the church and on fervent Christian living. Separatists had called for a religious reformation. The Moravians had longed for a restoration of religious fervor. The Quakers had protested spiritual superficiality and hypocrisy. The Baptists and other nonconformists had protested worldly practices in contemporary English Christianity and had worked for a deeper level of spiritual life.

Furthermore, the eighteenth century revival was sustained for more than a generation by the Methodist class meetings. John Wesley, with a genius for organization, saw that the spiritual lives of Christian people needed to be cared for in small groups. He inaugurated the class meeting that consisted of no more than twelve spiritually concerned people. These persons, under the direction of a carefully selected leader, met each week for personal spiritual examination, testimony and prayer.

The benefits of the small group meetings in early Methodism were immeasurable. At one time Wesley set forth their values as follows:

> Great and many are the advantages which have flowed from this closer union of believers with each other. They pray one for another that they might be healed of the faults they have confessed; and it was so. The chains were broken, the bands were burst asunder, and sin had no more dominion over them. Many were delivered from the temptations out of which, till then, they found no way of escape. They were built up in our most holy faith. They rejoiced in the Lord more abundantly. They were strengthened in love, and more effectually provoked to abound in every good work.[4]

At another time Wesley stated the values of the class meetings by saying that it could "scarcely be conceived what advantages had been reaped" from them.[5]

History gives a convincing testimony that small religious

---

[4] John Wesley, *Works* (New York: Mason and Lane, 1839), Vol. V, p. 183.
[5] *Ibid.*, Vol. II, p. 297.

groups are significant. It does not maintain narrowly that smallness in itself is a virtue but, on the other hand, it does not put a premium on large numbers. For some reason God has often chosen smaller groups through which to demonstrate his power. Sacred history has validated often the inspired word that one shall chase a thousand and two shall put ten thousand to flight (Deuteronomy 32:30; cf. Joshua 23:10). Likewise Paul's statement has been often proved, "God chose what is foolish in the world to shame the wise, God chose what is weak in the world to shame the strong, God chose what is low and despised in the world, even those things that are not, so that no man might boast in the presence of God." (RSV 1 Corinthians 1:27-29).

The Contemporary Significance of Smaller Churches

This generation is discovering the significance of smaller groups. Many disciplines are emphasizing that smaller groups are basic in the matter of effective living. For a generation sociology has stressed the importance of face-to-face relationships. Social psychology has emphasized the significance of social interaction in small groups. Psychologists and psychiatrists have stressed the value of meaningful interpersonal relationships. This viewpoint is of such importance that a "school" of psychology has arisen that is known as interpersonal psychology. Authorities in education, including religious educators, have drawn attention recently to the importance of group dynamics which may be defined as the motivation and influence that a group, usually smaller, exerts upon its members as they interact with each other.

Strain Wayland, an educator, believes that the present interest in smaller groups is a matter of high importance. He says that "when the academic history of the Post-War II period is written, considerable attention will be given to the widespread interest in small groups." [6]

---

[6] "Functional Roles of Small Groups in Larger Social Systems," *Teachers' College Record*, Vol. 55, p. 359.

The present interest in small groups has been motivated largely by the fact that American society has become increasingly impersonal. Many people now live in cities where attitudes are less friendly than in rural areas. Moreover, many of the small and friendly institutions of former generations have become impersonal. Large numbers of people now work in offices, factories, and shops that employ thousands of people. In contrast to former generations, a large part of the population trades at large department stores and supermarkets where they are not intimately acquainted with the clerks. Children are trained in large public schools instead of small one-room schools. Mass communications such as radio and television have done much to displace neighborly conversation. This generation is running short of opportunities for meaningful face-to-face contacts.

Many churches, particularly in cities, have been caught up in impersonal attitudes. Large crowds of worshipers go to hear a man preach and the people leave the house of God with little genuine friendly contact.

The smaller church, however, stands in contrast to the whole trend toward impersonal attitudes. It has all of the advantages of small groups. It is inherently a face-to-face institution. It is made up of people who know each other and who care about each other. It provides for a high rate of meaningful interaction between individuals. It has in it all of the elements for social interaction and effective influence that the social psychologists desire when they talk about group dynamics. It meets many of the basic wishes of men: acceptance, a sense of belonging, recognition, and love. The contemporary significance of the smaller church is great simply from social and psychological viewpoints.

The smaller church, characterized by personal and intimate attitudes, is able to make religion really meaningful to its adherents. It influences people deeply because of its intimate contacts. The pastor of one of America's large churches, Roy

A. Burkhart, says, "It becomes increasingly clear to anyone who is in the ministry that insight (on the part of the people) rarely grows as one talks to a large group. Lives are really changed in small groups and in counselling situations." [7] Burkhart refers to the ministry of Jesus in this regard, "The great changes that came over people through his ministry took place in his personal and small group contacts. He spoke to the multitudes but those who caught his spirit and were changed by him had either a personal or a very intimate relationship with him." [8]

It is recognized, of course, that large churches can be organized into small and effective groups. A few great churches have succeeded in doing this but many others have failed. In some churches 90% of the adult members do not participate regularly in church life other than in Sunday morning worship. The little church has the advantage along this line. It is inherently a group where personal and intimate attitudes prevail.

It is impossible to approximate the significance of smaller churches that actually undertake to develop Christians of deep devotion and of religious fervor. These churches are a leavening influence in major Christianity. They provide an inner strength to the whole Christian cause. Protestantism would be greatly impoverished without their example of spiritual earnestness.

George A. Buttrick believes that the hope of a genuine spiritual awakening in our day lies in the small religious groups. He says, "Real revivals have always begun in a little group that defied the values of the world and lived under a new and stringent discipline of life." [9] As noted above, history gives strong evidence that Buttrick is right in this viewpoint.

Elton Trueblood sees great contemporary significance in

[7] "The Man of the Month," *Pastoral Psychology*, IV (June, 1953), p. 66.

[8] *Ibid.*,, pp. 8, 66.

[9] In an address before the Chicago Sunday Evening Club, *The Christian Century* (February 29, 1956), p. 278.

small religious groups. He believes that they are the hope of the world—an alternative to the futility of the present age. Trueblood holds that Western civilization can be saved by "little redemptive societies" of spiritually concerned Christians. "The best chance for the renewal of the human spirit in the twentieth century, as in the first, lies in the formation of genuinely redemptive societies in the midst of ordinary society."[10] The minimum conditions for membership in such societies are: (1) thorough commitment to Christ; (2) willingness to witness to one's faith; (3) genuine fellowship; (4) a willingness to perform Christian work; and, (5) personal discipline.[11]

Smaller churches are needed today to help meet the challenge of America's awakening religious interest. The present resurgence of interest in religion confronts churches with the same general problem the public schools are facing. There are now more children to attend church schools. There are more young people for youth activities. There are more adults who have an interest in churchgoing. Most communities are not overchurched. They are actually underchurched in view of the fact that great numbers of people have not been reached for Christ. The churches in many American communities could not seat one-half the people, twelve years of age and older, if that many decided to attend service on the same Sunday morning.

Christians in little churches, even the smallest, need not be self-conscious or apologetic about the diminutive size of their groups. When God seeks to accomplish his purpose he, unlike man, does not start counting numbers. Judas Maccabeus, hard pressed in war by the Syrian hosts, gave eloquent expression to this truth. "There is no difference in the sight of heaven between saving through many or through few, for victory in

---

[10] Elton Trueblood, *Alternative to Futility* (New York: Harper and Brothers, 1948), p. 29.

[11] *Ibid.*, p. 61ff.

war does not depend upon the size of the force, but strength comes from heaven" (I Maccabees III, 18, 19). Christians in small religious groups today are in a great tradition that God has often used. God needs devout and spiritually profound groups today to give a clear witness of the gospel to this spiritually superficial age.

The Genius
of
Smaller Churches

2

The genius of smaller churches is seen in their capacity to promote the spiritual growth of their people. Smaller churches have a threefold advantage along this line. First, they can foster a genuine fellowship among all of their people. Secondly, they can enlist all of their people in personal participation in the life of the church. Thirdly, they are able to enlist, train and guide the majority of their members in active Christian service.

Spiritual Growth Through Fellowship

The Christian church arose as a fellowship and not as an organization. In the first portrayal of it, Luke tells us that "all who believed were together." He also says that the earliest Christians "were of one heart and soul, and no one said that any of the things which he possessed was his own, but they had everything in common" (RSV Acts 4:32). Here was an extraordinary fellowship, the quality of which the world had never seen. The believers demonstrated vividly their inner unity by a generous sharing of their goods.

The believers began early the practice of eating evening meals together, usually in the larger homes of the more well to do. In the earliest days, these fellowship meals were hearty and inclusive, ruling out economic superiority, social exclusiveness, racial intolerance, and intellectual snobbery. These evening, meals, later called *agapes,* continued to be distinguished by Christian fellowship and devotion.

Hearty fellowship among the Christians extended far beyond the Apostolic age. Justin, living in the middle of the second century, stated that the Christians were "constantly in touch with one another" (Apology, Vol. 1, p. 67). In still later periods the Christians had such genuine fellowship that Roman citizens exclaimed, "Behold how they love one another." Christian fellowship was so prominent in the second and third centuries that it won many converts. One of the strongest appeals that Christianity made to the outsider was its human warmth and the solidarity of its fellowship.[1]

The early Christians regarded fellowship as an important means of Christian growth. The earliest Christians, immediately after Pentecost, "devoted themselves to the apostles' teaching and fellowship, to the breaking of bread and the prayers" (RSV Acts 2:42). The writer of the Epistle to the Hebrews regarded continued Christian association as an important means to Christian maturity, "Let us consider how to stir up one another to love and good works, not neglecting to meet together, as is the habit of some, but encouraging one another" (RSV Hebrews 10:24, 25). Perhaps the low level of spiritual life among the Hebrew Christians had been occasioned in part because they had neglected Christian association. The writer believed that they must resume and maintain that association if they were to become mature Christians. In a later period, the writer of the Epistle of Barnabas warned Christians, living in an unfriendly world, against spiritual seclusion. "Keep not apart by yourselves in secret, as if you were already justified, but meet together and confer upon the common weal" (The Epistle of Barnabas IV:10). The first manual of the Christian church, The Didache, recognized that the Christians living in the second century needed a spiritual refreshment that comes through Christian association. It urged believers to "seek out every day the company of the saints, to

[1] A. B. MacDonald, *Christian Worship in the Primitive Church* (Edinburgh: T. & T. Clark, n.d.), p. 16.

be refreshed by their words" (Didache 4 :2).

John Morley says that it is "the little circle of his fellows that constitutes the world of a man" (On Compromise, p. 111). This was surely true of the early Christians. The small group of fellow Christians were the real world to early believers. It was in these groups that they really lived as they shared their interests, joys, failures and hopes. It is probable that some of the new converts were held loyal, during the early stages of their adhesion, as much by the ties of brotherhood as by the tie of devotion to the unseen Lord.[2]

Smaller churches today, like the Apostolic groups, are fellowships of friends. These churches approximate what sociologists call primary groups. The people in them have many meaningful face-to-face contacts that are based on appreciation and love. These groups are made up of people who know and accept each other. The members of them usually have a hearty sense of *belonging* for they are accepted for what they are. With a hearty "we" feeling there is little need for pretensions and airs. In such groups there is often a large degree of mutual confidence though the faults of each member are known and sometimes discussed. At their best, the people in smaller churches have a great deal of sympathetic understanding for one another. This is not pity but a sharing of ideas, ideals, sentiments, experiences and problems.

Let us observe more specifically that churches that actually give their people the opportunity for hearty and genuine fellowship provide a favorable climate for spiritual growth. Spiritual comradeship is essential in effective Christian living. John Wesley, originator of the Methodist class meetings, discovered this early. In his quest for soul peace, prior to 1738, an unknown person admonished him, "Sir, you wish to serve God and go to heaven? Remember you cannot serve Him alone. You must therefore find companions or make them; the Bible

---

[2] *Ibid.*, p. 16.

knows nothing of solitary religion." [3] The seventeenth century dramatist, George Chapman, recognized the beneficent influence of genuine affection:

> I tell you that love is nature's second sun,
> Causing a spring of virtues where it shines. [4]

Let us observe especially here how the mutual experiences of Christians in church life enrich corporate worship and make it an outstanding means of grace. Worship is normally at its best in a social-spiritual situation that is characterized by acquaintanceship, love and confidence. In such a situation there is a sense of fellowship though it is unspoken. A worshiper can sense the inarticulate concern and support of friends worshiping with him. Under such circumstances the worshiper, perhaps sorely tempted, finds it easy to accept God's understanding and love because he is surrounded by people who, he believes, understand and love him. On the other hand, he is helped to have confidence in God because he has confidence in trusted friends. Moreover, the pastor's message comes to him with increased relevance because he is with fellow worshipers who, he believes, accept the truth of the message. After the benediction has been pronounced, a friendly "God bless you," and a firm handclasp dramatize the sense of fellowship he experienced as he sat among friends who were concerned for him.

Furthermore, corporate worship in the little church is highly personalized, almost individualized, because the people are personally acquainted with their minister. He has called frequently in their homes. They have worked with him in church projects. Out of this intimate acquaintance the pastor preaches as a shepherd who knows his sheep as thoroughly as he knows his books. He speaks to them out of personal interest, as a friend and concerned counselor, and in no sense as a professional religionist.

[3] *Journal of John Wesley* (Eaton and Mains, n.d.), I, p. 469.

[4] *All Fools*, Acts I, Scene I, lines 98, 99.

Meaningful Christian association, wherever it is found, fosters spiritual growth. It increases spiritual interest, sharpens moral perceptions, and strengthens spiritual purposes. It kindles a desire for devotion and inspires a life of faith. It leads to a deepening commitment for Christian living and increases enthusiasm and zest for actually carrying out spiritual tasks. The contagion of ideals becomes effective in Christian fellowship and people find that their aspirations for Christ rise as they mingle with spirtually minded persons.

Some rural church sociologists have underestimated the spiritual values of fellowship when they have advised small churches to be closed and have suggested that the people drive to cities "where the churches are beautiful, ministers are able, and music is excellent." [5] Such a program has not worked, Clark maintains, and it has usually resulted in abandoned churches and godless communities. The rural people send their children out of their immediate communities to up-to-date consolidated schools and they drive many miles to modern supermarkets, but they want to worship with their friends. They regard spiritual fellowship more highly than erudite sermons and personal understanding more than beautiful music.

Spiritual Growth Through Personal Participation

The smaller church is a group of fellow Christians personally participating in spiritual matters. There are two reasons why smaller churches can enlist a large per cent of their members in active participation. First, the sense of fellowship makes it easy for the people to participate in all areas of church life. Secondly, the need for participants in smaller churches creates a situation of urgency that challenges the people to engage in the total program of the church.

Like a family, the smaller church is a group of interacting persons. In effective little churches, the people as a whole par-

---

[5] Neil M. Clark, "The Country Church Comes Back to Life," *Saturday Evening Post* (Nov. 20, 1954), p. 32.

ticipate in the Sunday school, the worship services, fellowship groups, revivals and other special meetings. Moreover, many of the people participate in prayer meetings, Bible studies, and special service activities. Such a high degree of general participation in the life of the church gives a unique character to the little congregation and it builds Christian character.

Little congregations often offer worshipers opportunities for public witnessing, extempore prayer and special singing. These opportunities are sometimes provided in the Sunday morning service but more often in the informal Sunday evening and midweek services. A part of the genius of the smaller church is seen in the large number of people who assemble at these informal meetings to engage in prayer, testimony, and group discussion of spiritual things.

Regular participation in the program of the church builds spiritual life through loyalty to the church. An actual sharing of activity creates a kind of group magnetism that keeps the participants loyal. The group magnetism arises because the people have a *sense of belonging* and they feel *wanted* and *needed*. These interior incentives make unnecessary artificial exterior motivations such as coaxing people to attend. Furthermore, they contribute to the development of Christian character. Spiritual life flourishes when people really identify themselves with a group of spiritually minded Christians and are loyal to it.

John Wesley realized clearly the spiritual values of personal participation in the worship of small groups. He limited his class meetings to twelve persons so that there might be general participation. Many historians see the very genius of early Methodism in these small groups of worshipers who shared their experiences with each other.

In the recent past the writer had an extended conversation with old friends, a husband and wife, who had been brought up in smaller churches. These people, however, had spent most of their adult lives in larger congregations. During our conversation I asked my friends what unique and abiding value they now saw in their smaller home churches.

The woman spoke first and stated that she continued to appreciate the sense of fellowship of the people of the little church during her youth. She made this more pointed by saying that she recalled that her mother went often to the church services heavily burdened and greatly distressed. During some of those meetings, informal in nature, her mother had an opportunity to express herself freely in testimony and prayer about some of the burdens that she was bearing. At other times she requested the prayers of the group, always being assured that she was among people who really cared.

"I have gone with my mother to those meetings when she was greatly discouraged," this friend said, "and I have seen her return home as if she were a new person. That is the value of smaller churches."

Spiritual Growth Through Christian Service

The Apostolic churches were groups of functioning saints. In a superbly fine figure of speech, Paul compares a local Christian church to the human body. As every part of the body performs its unique function, so every member of the church performs the work for which he is fitted (Romans 12:4, 5). Moffatt translates vividly a portrayal of the effective working of an early Christian church.

> Our talents differ with the grace that is given us; if the talent is that of prophecy, let us employ it in proportion to our faith; if it is practical service let us mind our service; the teacher must mind his teaching, the speaker his words of counsel; the contributor must be liberal, the superintendent must be in earnest, the sick visitor must be cheerful (Romans 12:6-8).

One reason for the strength of the early church is seen in the fact that the believers generally took part in Christian service. It seems that all believers accepted responsibility for the work of the Kingdom. The cleavage between clergy and laymen was unknown in the earliest period and believers generally used their gifts in the various ministries of the churches. Emil Brunner suggests that the "active-expending and the passive-receiving parts of the church" did not appear until later.

The problem of enlisting laymen in Christian service is an important problem today. The problem is twofold: opportunities of Christian service must be found, and secondly, the people must be interested. Clayton Luce, Christian evangelist and keen observer, once said that pastors today have no greater problem than that of finding opportunities of service for their people. It is quite understandable that pastors of smaller churches can solve this problem more readily than those of large congregations.

Active Christian service is uniquely important as a means of Christian growth. This is because Christian experience is a *life* to be lived and not simply the attainment of religious knowledge or the acceptance of a creed. The Christian life consists largely of attitudes, sentiments, ideals, faith, and habits instead of an accumulation of religious knowledge. The former cannot be attained alone by hearing sermons or by reading religious books. The educational principle "learning by doing" is valid here.

Froebel emphasized the importance of action in education. He gave his teachers the following statement as a motto to hang on the walls of their studies: "All growth must come from the voluntary action of the child himself." Froebel's principle has relevance for the development of Christian character in all age groups.

Smaller churches are able to bring a larger per cent of their people into firsthand contact with Christian reality through active service. To use an educational figure, the little church offers better laboratory opportunities for Christian growth. This directed laboratory experience is important as a supplement to the sermon. It is as significant, perhaps, as laboratory experience to the student of science. Very frequently, preachers, like teachers, have found that people do not learn well by public discourses alone. Congregations of people can assimilate bodies of religious knowledge without changing their attitudes, ideals and habits.

A college professor of sociology, early in one semester, gave his students an examination designed to measure their proneness toward racial bigotry. During the remainder of the semester the students took an extended course of lectures and readings that dealt with the scientific facts of racial differences. The course showed clearly that many of the current notions about people of other races were without foundation. Near the end of the course the professor gave two more examinations. One was designed to test the students' knowledge of race relations and the other to test their attitudes toward people of other races. Most of the students passed the first examination but showed little change of attitude on the second. They learned the facts but they kept their old prejudices and attitudes. How often has this happened with preaching!

Trueblood believes that any group that can enlist the active participation and service of all of its members is significant and that it will be a dynamic force in society. Using the figure of a ship he says, "Make all, within your society (or church), members of the crew and permit no passengers." [6]

Let the people in every little church recognize that smaller churches have a genius for developing spiritual living. Let them recognize, also, that this genius is akin to that of the Apostolic church and, moreover, that it has timeless significance. Appreciating these facts, let the people in smaller churches face courageously the problems that inhere in the diminutive size of their groups and let them build a program that capitalizes on their areas of strength.

---

[6] *Alternative to Futility* (New York: Harper and Brothers, 1948), p. 74.

3 The Tendency Toward Introversion

Like persons, local churches are sometimes introvertive. Following the introvertive pattern in human personality, these churches turn their interests and their energies inwardly upon themselves. They are concerned primarily with their own affairs. Sometimes they devote most of their attention to spiritual introspection which results in a neglect of spiritual expression in their communities.

Introvertive churches usually have greater interests in religious abstractions than in Christian action. They tend to be overly reflective, introspective, and mystical. They sometimes have an overly exclusive interest in the theological content of religion. I have attended ministers' conferences in which the preachers discussed with enthusiasm certain obscure theological concepts and hypothetical philosophical propositions, but they showed little interest in principles of evangelistic outreach or local church effectiveness. I have known churches that had a high degree of interest in peripheral religious concepts but little interest in assignments of actual Christian work and service to their communities.

Pronounced examples of ecclesiastical introversion are seen in churches that withdraw from the life of their communities. They do not cooperate with other churches nor with community welfare agencies. Usually they are unconcerned with effective means of community outreach. They are in effect "little islands of holiness in a great sea of worldliness," and they have very little impact on this "sea of worldliness."

The Struggle for Survival

The struggle for survival tends to develop introversion in institutions as well as in individuals. A man in a hazardous situation, for instance, thinks primarily of saving himself. A poor man struggling to make a living gives less attention to others than his affluent neighbor who has considerable wealth. Likewise, the smaller church with pressing needs and limited finance frequently develops an introvertive way of life.

In a survey of churches in one denomination, J. A. Robb, a district superintendent, found that the per capita giving was about the same for the smaller as for the larger congregations. The people in the smaller churches, however, gave much less for missions, Christian education, community welfare projects, and other benevolences. The restricted range of giving on the part of the people in the smaller churches was occasioned, quite understandably, by the urgent needs of their local groups. It is important to note, nevertheless, that that situation makes for narrowed interests and it can confirm an introvertive pattern of life for a church.

Moreover, the struggle for survival often causes inferiority feelings in local churches. A number of factors are involved when this happens. Limited size and resources cause people to feel that their church is "poor." Lack of impressive buildings makes them self-conscious of their limitations. Lack of status in their communities makes them apologetic. Lack of achievement occasions a sense of frustration. All such introvertive appraisals of small congregations usually result in inferiority feelings.

Inferiority complexes are as damaging to churches as to persons. They hinder vision and obscure challenging opportunities for service. They undercut self-confidence and no captivating program is launched. They diminish enthusiasm and activities are carried on in an unimaginative manner. They reduce vigor and projects are not launched with strength. Churches with inferiority complexes are usually timid and overly cautious, lack-

31

ing a spirit of adventure. They often manifest fear of a sinful world and withdraw from it. Their cooperation with other churches is often hesitating and ineffective.

The struggle for survival, along with inferiority feelings, often involves smaller churches in other problems of self evaluation. Struggling churches are likely to exaggerate points of superiority they actually possess as a means of compensation for their limitations. This is done most frequently in the area of spiritual life, for, as noted before, many smaller churches do excel here. It is easy for a smaller church to compensate for other limitations by overemphasizing its own spirituality. The people may say to themselves, "We do not have a large congregation or a lovely sanctuary, but we are *spiritual*." Such an attitude, perhaps innocently made, appears as a "holier than thou" attitude to others.

Attitudes of spiritual superiority have a twofold effect. In the first place, they hinder further spiritual growth. Spiritually satisfied persons and institutions are unlikely to spend effort in further development. The truly spiritual person, like the real scholar, is always mindful of the possibilities of further achievement. The same rule holds for churches. Secondly, assumptions of spiritual superiority estrange people from their communities. Most people like holier-than-thou groups as little as they like conceited persons.

The struggle for survival causes some smaller churches to become egocentric because of their fear of extinction. Egocentricity is frequently an exaggerated form of introversion. It suggests complete concern with self. Home missionary boards confirm the egocentric tendencies of struggling congregations by giving financial assistance to them. Such assistance often represents a projection of the board's own egocentricity. The denominational board considers the local mission church of its denomination of inherent worth and it paternalistically gives to help maintain the congregation's *status quo* and, also, to help maintain the respect of the denomination in the community.

The little church, encouraged in its egocentricity, accepts the subsidy as a pampered boy takes a handout from an overly indulgent father. Where such attitudes prevail, the subsidy is not only wasted but the congregation is harmed. The church comes to feel that there is little need of exercising initiative as long as the funds of a generous mission board seem assured. Every Home Mission Board should inquire carefully into the attitudes of small congregations before grants are made. Will the proposed grant help or hinder the congregation? Is the congregation eagerly anticipating the day when it can be self-sustaining? Will the grant assist the church to evangelize its community or will the money be used to maintain its *status quo?* If the church receives the subsidy for the latter purpose, its status isn't worth maintaining at *"quo."*

Smaller churches must do more than struggle for survival. They must grow. Even here there lurks a temptation to introversion. The desire to grow may become so strong that the church will ask, "What opportunities does the community offer for my growth?" Such a question inverts the impulse of the gospel. It has the flavor of the egocentric. The sincere Christian congregation asks, "What needs does the community have which the church can meet?"

Pampering the Saints

There are churches that choose the introvertive pattern of life so that they may devote most of their attention to perfecting the Christian experiences of their people. Ernst Troeltsch maintains that the churches of many of the smaller denominations, which he calls "sects," are motivated primarily by this impulse. He believes that these churches view the matter of "perfecting the saints" as their chief end rather than the task of redeeming sinners and society as a whole. Because of their interest in deep spirituality, these churches frequently reject contemporary culture and retreat from the world. This estranges them in their communities which in turn strengthens their introvertive impulses. Such churches often become specialists in the art of perfecting the saints but they frequently have a marked deficiency in influencing the world.

The life of the introvertive church consists primarily in religious services designed for the culture of Christians. If evangelistic services are carried on there is little response from the community because there has been little personal outreach or community action on the part of the congregation. The evangelistic services become then, of necessity, meetings for the further spiritual development of believers.

Highly introvertive churches with an overly exclusive concern about their own perfection often develop a type of institutional hypochondria. Hypochondria in churches, as in persons, represents an exaggerated anxiety about health. In such groups the people are highly self-conscious about their spiritual welfare. Many of the members are "constitutional doubters" with little capacity for faith and confident Christian living. Recognition of spiritual inadequacy in ecclesiastical hypochondria is not of the healthful type. It does not lead to growth or creative action.

It should be noted that the impulse to withdraw from the world is inherent in Christianity and it has been demonstrated since the early days of the church. By the fourth century the monastic impulse was strong and many of the best Christians went into seclusion so that they might perfect their own lives. In some eras of the church, particularly in the Middle Ages, the monastic impulse was so strong that the world was deprived of the active services of most of the devout Christians. The impulse to withdraw into introversion has been strong even in Protestantism. It is true that we have not had monasteries but we have had religious colonies. Presently, the introvertive impulse is expressed by a lack of concern for the world while attention is devoted to the development of personal piety. It is found sometimes among groups that correctly put a strong emphasis on full commitment to Christ believing it is better to have one hundred per cent of one man than ten per cent of ten men. This emphasis must not make the church forget the world.

Elmer Homrighausen, in speaking of introvertive churches, says,

> They often fossilized and immunized themselves in the process, and, by failing to be concerned with the real situation of modern man have been just as guilty in deserting the present scene and alienating the gospel from the world (as compromised churches). They have saved themselves but in the process have not only lost the world, but have falsified the living truth of Christianity as well. No church will be saved by becoming a hermit; it is saved by faith and incarnate love.[1]

Some readers may believe at this point that we wish less attention devoted to the development of personal Christian experience but such is not the case. No thoughtful person could wish for a weakened program for the development of Christian character when he considers the low level of spiritual life in American Protestantism. We wish that all churches might have a broader approach in their work that would result in the development of deeper piety and a more effective outreach to the world.

This is not an "either-or" matter. It is not a matter of spiritual introversion or religious extroversion. The church does not have to choose between an intensive or an extensive program. It may have both.

The facts are, of course, that many churches fail along this line. We have noted the failure of many smaller churches in the matter of introversion. Contrariwise, many large congregations have failed at the point of spiritual superficiality. The latter have engaged themselves in a busy round of community activities, many of which have a minimum of spiritual significance.

Let introvertive churches accept the fact that God himself

---

[1] Elmer Homrighausen, *Choose Ye This Day* (Philadelphia: Westminster, 1943), p. 39. Used by permission.

seems little interested in tiny isolated colonies of holy people who are unconcerned about others. Such churches should know that spirituality has little value if it is unrelated to Christian witnessing and Christian action. Piety becomes uninviting if it is unconcerned with impious things. It is really unhealthy if it is unconcerned with Christian service.

Let the introvertive church recognize that Christian action is a means of grace. As a matter of fact, Christian character cannot be developed genuinely apart from active Christian service. Most Christians grow more in an evening of sincere lay evangelistic visitation than in an evening of religious meditation. The hearty protest of a community evil sometimes occasions more Christian growth than the reading of a good religious book.

Spiritual Hospitality

Hospitality is rooted in sharing and it is, at heart, a Christian grace. In its primary sense, of course, it refers to sharing the comforts of one's home with guests.

The early Christians emphasized the grace of hospitality. The primitive believers were urged to share the comforts of their homes with others, particularly with travelers, whether friends or strangers. The Pastoral Epistles state that one of the qualifications of pastors, called bishops in that day, was hospitality (I Timothy 3:2; Titus 1:8). A qualification of widows who served as church workers was an attitude of hospitality (I Timothy 5:10). Paul urged all Christians to "practice hospitality" (Romans 12:13). The Epistle of Hebrews counsels all believers to "not forget to be hospitable to strangers for by being so, some, without knowing it, have had angels as their guests" (Goodspeed's translation, Hebrews 13:2).

The term, hospitality, however, is used in broader senses than the entertainment of guests. There is an intellectual hospitality that refers to the generous sharing of knowledge on the part of an informed person. "The mind has various hospitalities to offer." [2] There is also a spiritual hospitality that refers to a generous sharing of the riches the Christian has found in Christ.

Spiritual hospitality stands in contrast to spiritual introversion. It suggests an outreach to others rather than an overemphasis on one's own Christian experience. It is rooted in the genuine concern for other people's spiritual welfare. It assumes an attitude of Christian friendliness and an ability to converse naturally about spiritual things. It is often seen in a natural and spontaneous witnessing for Christ.

Today's spiritual hospitality usually starts when a Christian offers to share his church privileges with others. This involves, most simply, an invitation to another to attend Sunday school or church services. The invitation may be made graciously, with genuine spiritual hospitality, or ungraciously. The genuinely hospitable invitation emphasizes the values that one can have in worship, the study of God's Word, and Christian fellowship. It is an appeal for the outsider to partake of these. The ungracious invitation is rooted in egocentricity. It is sometimes made as follows: "Will you come to my Sunday school next Sunday? We want a record attendance." Such an invitation is really rooted in inhospitality. It asks a favor of another, either for himself or for his church. Sometimes one's friends actually respond to such an invitation in deference to the one making it, but it does little to kindle genuine spiritual interest. It is true that this type of church invitation has certain short-time values that inhere in the enthusiasm of the situation but no church can prosper in the long run unless there are more basic spiritual elements in its promotion. Sometimes spiritual inhospitality is shown by an invitation to others to attend church that includes an implicit reprimand, "You should go to church." This type of invitation often causes offense and it does more harm than good.

[2] *Spectator* (June 14, 1890).

Moreover, there should be hospitality in the house of God when people come to worship. Upon entering the sanctuary, people should receive a genuine welcome and be made to feel at ease.

It is usually the ushers that welcome people to the house of God. These men, if well trained for their work, do this with a splendid Christian courtesy. Effective ushers are friendly and they greet people with a smile, a friendly handshake, or a "Good morning." In their friendliness, effective ushers are not gushy. They do not act as though they are tickled that certain people, perhaps new to the church, have come to worship. The matter of greeting people at the church is far more important than most smaller churches realize. It is comparable to welcoming one's friends or strangers when they come to his home. There are people who have something of the same sense of strangeness in walking into a strange church that they would have in walking unbidden into another person's home.

It should be emphasized that the hospitality of the Church depends upon all of the members and not only upon ushers. The regular worshipers should show a genuine Christian friendliness to those who are new and to those who do not attend regularly. A hearty handshake and a friendly word after the benediction do much to convince people of the church's interest in them. Many times it is the smaller so-called "friendly" churches that are most unfriendly to newcomers. In such churches I have seen small cliques of people busily engaged in conversation with one another, following the benediction, while newcomers left the church unnoticed.

Finally, it must be recognized that the heart of spiritual hospitality is seen in the natural and spontaneous sharing of the gospel. This goes much further than inviting people to church and showing a friendly attitude toward them in the house of God. This type of Christian concern is an every-day affair and it is expressed in the common walks of life. It is basically different from organized lay visitation evangelism, for in this type of witnessing the Christian is ever alert to opportunities to share the gospel in any place and at any time.

The early Christians excelled in this matter and one of the important reasons for the growth of the early church is seen in the spontaneous witnessing of the believers. The desire to witness to Christ was so strong that the early Christians could not be silent. On being commanded to speak no more about Christ, Peter and John exclaimed, "For we cannot but speak the things we have seen and heard" (Acts 4:20). When the Church's first persecution scattered all of the believers from Jerusalem, excepting the Apostles, they went everywhere telling the good news of Christ (Acts 8:4). The early Christians put in practice Jesus' command, "Ye shall be witnesses unto me" (Acts 1:8). In those early days it seems that every believer had a hearty word on his lips for Christ.

One of the reasons why those early Christians were so effective in their natural witness to others was because they knew that they had found the answer to human misery. To appreciate properly the importance of this fact we must recall that the people of the first century were unhappy, frustrated, and troubled. For three hundred years the philosophers had looked for the answer to the human plight. Greek philosophy had become a "way-of-life" movement and the best minds of the age had sought to solve the problem of confident and effective living. The answer had been revealed to the believers by Christ. He was the Way, the Truth, and the Life. The most simple believer now possessed the answer for which profound philosophers had sought. To be quiet about Christ, who was their answer, would have been a betrayal to their fellow men. They had the Desire of Ages and they shared Him with others.

The early Christians knew the secret of spiritual hospitality. They helped people in the perplexing problems of life by sharing the good news of Christ. The church has never found a more effective means.

Christians today have as much to share with troubled people

as the early Christians had. They can commend faith to the fearful, confidence to the frustrated, and healing to the sick. They can offer Christ's wisdom to the perplexed and their own Christian fellowship to the lonely. They have the message of divine forgiveness for the guilt-oppressed and they can assure the hopeless of God's concern. Christians today can share the riches of God's Word with others and they can point them to Christ in prayer.

Many churches fail in spiritual hospitality because of one of two extremes. First, some churches fail because of a lack of genuine spiritual concern for the lives of people. Their Christian hospitality is shallow. Their overt desire to gain another attendant or another member for their church overshadows their spiritual concern for the people they try to win. Such a type of hospitality is rooted in ecclesiastical egocentricity.

On the other hand, many evangelical and evangelistic Christians approach this matter from another extreme position. They have concern for people because they want to save a soul from hell. This is an ultimate concern, of course, but it frequently has little appeal to those who are being contacted. The perplexities of the present life are more real and urgent to most people than the fear of future punishment. Inasmuch as this is the case, Christians must show their interest in the present problems of people and they must offer to share generously their spiritual insight in the solution of these perplexities. The present interest in life-situation preaching has demonstrated the value of starting where people actually are.

How shall a church save itself from introversion? By losing itself in generous service. As it does this it acquires a magnetism that draws people to it. Let it view its task as sowing the gospel seed by all waters.

Jesus gave us the law for spiritual achievement in the Kingdom. This law is applicable to both individuals and institutions. "For whosoever will save his life shall lose it; and whosoever will lose his life for my sake shall find it" (Matthew 16:25). George Buttrick aptly comments on this passage:

This is cosmic truth. It is true of health; health fussily safeguarded becomes hypochondria, but health expended in energy may grow. It is true of the harvest; the seed must die to live. It is true of the church; it dies if it seeks its own power and it lives if it proclaims the gospel.[8]

The way for the struggling church to overcome its introversion is by effective service. Let it rally its members and take the gospel to every unevangelized home in its community. Let it deliberately recruit the unreached children and youth and faithfully teach them the Word of God. Let its members visit the sick, bear the burdens of the weak, and minister to the brokenhearted. In doing these things that church shall save itself from introversion and it shall be saved to the Kingdom.

[8] *The Interpreters Bible* (Nashville: Abingdon-Cokesbury, 1951), Matthew 16:25.

Maintaining Morale

A denominational leader concerned primarily with smaller churches declares, "The matter of morale is our number one problem. There are many problems but this one eclipses all of them." In a survey of district superintendents in both a large and a small denomination 75% of these leaders declared that low morale was so frequently found in small churches that it constituted "a primary problem." These superintendents supervised the work of hundreds of smaller congregations in several states. Pastors of smaller churches likewise stated that low morale was found in at least three out of four of the smaller congregations and that it was one of their greatest problems. There are several elements in the inherent situation of the small church that makes morale a basic problem.

We use the term *morale* to suggest the *esprit de corps* of a group. It is composed of several substantial elements including confidence, zeal and enthusiasm. It is expressed in wholehearted loyalty for and cooperation in a common cause. It is an intangible but nonetheless a pervasive force. Its presence or absence makes for the success or the failure of a group.

Morale *per se* is something that cannot be added to a group in a hasty or arbitrary manner. It is not put on by an act of the will or by a vote of the official board. A great athletic director, "Hurry-up" Yost, used to tell his teams, "You don't put morale on like a coat. You build it day by day." [1] Morale

---

[1] *Time* (November 7, 1955), p. 93.

is the end product of healthful conditions that characterize a group. It is the healthful expression of vigorous life. Morale is to the mind what conditioning is to the athlete's body. Good morale is good conditioning of the inner man.

Importance of Morale

Morale is an essential factor for successful groups. "A church can accomplish anything it wishes if it has morale," said a denominational secretary of Sunday schools. This splendid overstatement is basically true. "Once achieved, proper morale becomes the rich soil in which activities flourish through the eager participation of the individuals concerned."[2] Every year hundreds of churches in America, large and small, demonstrate the value of morale by phenomenal achievements that were based on confidence, zeal and enthusiasm.

The importance of morale can be seen more clearly by looking at the effects of lowered morale. With lowered morale a group is in a poor state of health and unequipped for vigorous action. There is a loss of the will to succeed. There comes an adjustment to the *status quo* which is frequently an adjustment to mediocrity.

There is a loss of vision and vigor with lowered morale. The pastor himself loses enthusiasm and zeal after several months or years of unproductive labor. The laymen develop ecclesiastical inferiority feelings and become apologetic about their "little church." Furthermore, having seen the failure of many attempts at building up the congregation, the lay people sometimes become skeptical about the validity of the mission of their church. After this has happened they become dull and incredulous concerning every valid church plan and program.

A newly appointed pastor was commending enthusiastically the matter of lay visitation to build up his church and Sunday school attendance. His enthusiasm was met by an incredulous

---

[2] David I. Satlow, "What is Your Departmental M. Q. (Morale Quotient)?" *The Journal of Educational Sociology,* Vol. 27, (March, 1954), p. 239.

attitude on the part of his board. One board member volunteered, "We tried that when your predecessor was here and it didn't work."

As a district superintendent I recall suggesting to a lay leader of a church that his congregation should plan to have a revival meeting. This good man, the best in the church, said, "Must we have a revival meeting again? We have had so many and nothing has come of them."

With lowered morale the smaller church is threatened with a type of institutional neurasthenia. Becoming chronically weary, it loses the vision of its opportunities and a sense of futility develops concerning its program. Sometimes those who have supported it strongly come to question the validity of their investments. Worship services are abandoned by many and others attend out of the sense of obligation. Duties become perfunctory and are accomplished with little expectancy and faith. A crippling sense of inertia annuls the effectiveness of every endeavor.

The churches to which The Epistle to the Hebrews is addressed are New Testament examples of churches with low morale. The Christians in these churches were questioning the validity of the gospel; they had lost sight of their great mission; and they were forsaking the assembling of themselves together. Howard Kuist, Professor of Biblical Theology at Princeton Theological Seminary, used to refer to these Hebrew churches as representing many modern congregations. "They were not exactly dead; they were just 'dead tired.'"

The Problem of Status

The status that a church has in a community is often an important element in its morale. A church that is well known and widely accepted has an advantage in morale building. Usually a number of things contribute to its favorable status including architecture, the standing of its members, and the distinction of its minister. The smaller church often lacks all of these status-giving elements.

44

Many people derive considerable personal status, and hence morale, by belonging to groups with high community standing. Several years ago, as pastor in Pomona, California, I was making a survey of the community in which my church was located. When calling at the door of a modest home, a woman told me that she "belonged to the church where all the lawyers belonged." It was obvious that her ecclesiastical association with the lawyers gave her a heightened sense of worth and considerable confidence in her church. Another woman, in the same survey, expressed enthusiasm and confidence because she belonged to the church "where all the rich people go." This was a different church from the former, and I did not seek to learn how the lawyers got separated from the rich, but she, too, had a heightened sense of worth because of her fraternity with the well-to-do. Her enthusiasm for her church contributed to its morale.

The need for a heightened personal status is so great that some people are psychologically and spiritually unprepared to belong to smaller congregations. Upon moving to a city, they drive past a small congregation of their own denomination and go to one with a higher standing in the city.

Crowds give a church status. In a democracy many persons believe that a large crowd is a convincing vote of confidence in an institution while a small group indicates a losing cause. Moreover, a large congregation inspires enthusiasm and confidence. Some of the same elements that are found in the stadium exist in the sanctuary. Most people are more enthusiastic about a football game as they sit in a crowd of 50,000 than they would be in a small group of fifty.

Smaller churches sometimes have a lowered morale because they become over-self-conscious about their diminutive size. The pastor of a little congregation, for instance, may become acutely aware of the smallness of his little flock when some of his clerical brethren speak of their membership rolls and budgets at the ministerial association meetings. His own morale is lowered when he compares his pitifully modest salary with those of the more prosperous brethren. Small churches often interpret or misinterpret, as the case may be, the attitudes of larger congregations in their conferences and they come to regard themselves as a part of the "poor relations" of their denomination. General church officers, district superintendents, and pastors of larger churches sometimes unwittingly add to this sense of frustration by indicating that the small churches are "problem children." The "problem child" attitude is unfortunate and detrimental whether found in churches or in youngsters.

Avoiding Personality Tensions

Morale problems frequently arise because of the stresses and tensions that grow out of the close interpersonal relationships of small groups. H. P. Douglas exaggerates and oversimplifies the situation when he states that life in a smaller church is characterized by "captiousness and censoriousness." [3] He believes that, "Ugly dispositions and inability to enjoy or reflect the gospel are the almost certain consequences of smaller churches." [4]

While we may accept Douglas' viewpoint as an overstatement, we should be frank in observing that it is in the smaller groups that stresses are most likely to occur. The loves and resentments of little groups are intense. The university professor, for instance, is more likely to have stresses with the men in his own department than with other people in the university with whom he has only casual contact. His close interpersonal relationships with the men he sees often can give rise to misunderstandings.

The smaller church is subject to personality stresses, also, because maladjusted people sometimes seek out a small church so that they may receive added attention on the part of the pastor and members. These people often wish places of leadership

---

[3] "A New Chapter in Cooperative Churchmanship," *Christendom*, Vol. 7 (Winter, 1942), p. 96.
[4] *Ibid.,* p. 96.

to satisfy their unhappy egos. They are ofteri easily given to offense and resentments. If they are promoted to places of leadership their influence is almost certain to be disruptive.

Personality tensions and clashes represent an antithesis to the fellowship that characterizes small groups and the stresses are particularly detrimental to the morale of a little church. They tend to involve the whole congregation, whereas in a larger church differences of opinion often affect only one club or group. Relationships are so intimate in a small church that personality clashes frequently divide whole congregations, sometimes along the line of blood relationship. In a large church when a person becomes disgruntled in one group, he may move to a similar group in the same church. In smaller congregations the disgruntled person transfers his membership to another church or, worse still, he continues his disruptive influence in the group he dislikes.

The leaders in a small church must be people of constructive personalities if stresses and tensions are to be kept at a minimum, and morale is to be maintained at a high level. This means that both the pastor and lay officers must be creative and constructive in their attitudes. In a survey of 1,784 public school teachers in 43 states it was found that one of the most important factors in teacher "satisfaction" or morale was a "dynamic and stimulating leadership by the principal." [5]

Psychologists have pointed out that there are two types of personalities, the constructive and the destructive. The constructive personality is one that maintains positive and confident attitudes toward other people and he helps them to be confident and enthusiastic themselves. In the presence of such a leader, whether pastor or lay leader, ideas flow freely and service is spontaneous and joyous. The destructive personality is otherwise. He is uncertain, inadequate, frustrated, and often highly critical of others. He is frequently rigid and negativistic, being

[5] Frances S. Chase, "Factors for Satisfaction in Teaching," *Phi Deltan Kappan,* Vol. 33 (November, 1951), 127, 128.

able to observe one flaw in a whole galaxy of virtues. In the presence of such a person ideas come slowly, expression is faltering, and service is ineffective.

There are three things that constructive leaders do that are significant in raising the morale of groups. These results are seen in both ministerial and lay leadership within churches.

First, constructive leaders inspire enthusiasm. To use Lechy's phrase, every leader needs to represent "disciplined enthusiasm" about his program and with his fellow workers. Lechy used this term in reference to the total spirit of early Christianity.[*] It is equally important in contemporary church life. It is true that "no virtue is safe that is without enthusiasm." No movement can prosper without enthusiasm. It is as important in church life as in any other activity.

Secondly, the constructive personality raises the morale of the group by recognizing merit in others. He is generous in his approval of the tasks that have been done well. He himself is well adjusted and he does not find it necessary to minimize others or to withhold merited acknowledgment in a vain effort to raise his own self esteem and status. The constructive leader has faith in his fellow men and he is hearty in his recognition of the good work they are doing.

The matter of the recognition of good service is more important in morale building than most leaders think. The matter of morale has been studied extensively in industry and many of the studies rate recognition of work done at or near the top of all the factors making for good morale. Baring, Langfeld, and Weld, for instance, report a study in which credit for work done was regarded by employees as the most important factor in their working conditions. It was rated higher than interesting work, fair play, promotion on merit, job security, good physical working conditions and counsel on personal problems. It is interesting to note that the employers of the above men-

[*] Wm. E. H. Lechy, *History of European Morals,* 6th Edition, Vol. I (New York: Appleton), p. 389.

tioned employees did not regard "credit for work done" as important. They rated it seventh in the list of eight factors significant in morale building.[7] Perhaps even ministers have been equally insensitive to how much people crave recognition of merit.

Recognition of merit, however, is a matter that works both ways. The minister himself and his lay leaders need the appreciation of the congregation in order to maintain their own morale. The leader in a camp of conscientious objectors was being visited by military inspectors during World War II. The inspectors asked what was being done to raise morale. The leader of the camp, recognizing the difficulty of the morale problem, replied, "I know I am responsible for the morale of this camp, but who is responsible for my morale?" Perhaps many preachers have asked that same question when the going was hard.

Thirdly, constructive leaders are able to work with people who have a tendency to cause stress in groups because they understand some of the psychological factors involved. They know that certain people oppose the majority opinion because of a deeply seated negativism, perhaps rooted in childhood. They know also that some people cling to traditional ways of doing things because of temperamental reasons. On the other hand, they recognize that other people champion the new ideas because of temperamental and emotional factors. They understand that a few persons were deprived of love in early childhood and are thus unable either to give or to receive genuine love. They know well that there are people with inferiority feelings who compensate with dominant and arbitrary attitudes. Having a basic understanding of human nature, the constructive leaders accept the maladjusted persons instead of becoming highly critical of them. They work with them, as far as pos-

---

[7] *Foundations of Psychology* (New York: John Wiley and Sons, 1948), p. 483.

sible, instead of rejecting them. This procedure reduces the number of stress situations in a group and it builds morale.

Getting a Sense of Achievement

The morale of smaller churches is often lowered by a lack of objective success. It is readily recognized that a sense of achievement is usually necessary for a spirit of enthusiasm and confidence. A winning football team has higher morale than one that has lost several successive games. An army that has several victories to its credit usually has higher morale than one that has been steadily defeated. As "nothing succeeds like success" so few things are more important to high morale than success-mindedness.

The smaller church that has had little growth in attendance or membership over a period of years is almost certain to have a morale problem. A part of the reason for this is seen in the American assumption that institutions, like babies, should grow. The church that is located in a growing community, and perhaps near one or more growing churches, is likely to develop a sense of defeat if it is unable to observe some measurable gains. If it actually avoids a sense of defeat it may adopt an "holier than thou" attitude and become ecclesiastically smug. When this happens, the latter end is worse than the former.

The evangelistic church is particularly hard pressed at the point of showing continuous growth. Its primary purpose is to see souls saved. Unlike less evangelistic churches, it cannot be satisfied with only a program of Christian education and worship. It is forced to acknowledge certain degrees of defeat if there are not converts accompanied by growth in attendance and membership. It is a well known fact that this impulse for success is so great in some local churches that, lacking converts of their own, they turn to proselyting.

There are churches that need nothing more than they need a sense of achievement. A sense of achievement would enable them to undertake greater tasks. Robert Edwin Peary has been quoted as saying while on his expedition to the North Pole, "the exhilaration of success lent wings to our sorely battered feet."

In situations where morale is low because of little achievement, pastors and official boards must canvass thoroughly the needs of their communities and the opportunities for their churches. Upon finding needs for their services they should lead their churches in concentrated efforts to accomplish the tasks with marked success. This has been done often in building up Sunday schools. Frequently an aggressive pastor and an awakened board have led the way in enlisting Sunday school members so that the church school showed marked growth in a few months. This kind of achievement gives courage to the people and equips them for bigger undertakings.

A few years ago a young minister went to a little and disheartened church in California. Morale was low and the people were apathetic about their church program. The young pastor observed that the younger people of the community had little opportunity for wholesome recreation. Under his leadership his church inaugurated a program of Christian recreation on a newly constructed playground situated on the expansive church grounds. The success of this program greatly heartened the church people for they had the sense of accomplishing something for the young people. With renewed vision the church then reorganized its Sunday school and many of the younger people enrolled as members and attended regularly. This led to increased evangelistic efforts and a large group of the youth was converted. The church was soon filled with hearty worshipers and it took on new life. Churches, much like individuals, can be born again.

Frequently, however, smaller achievements have raised the morale of congregations. Some discouraged congregations have obtained new confidence because a new coat of paint was applied to a weather-beaten exterior or to smoked-up walls inside the sanctuary. At other times artful landscaping has revived the confidence and morale of a disheartened people. As a matter of fact, all needed physical improvements have a morale-raising potential. To some readers this may seem like running "along the little side hills of success," as Frank Moore Colby once said, but such efforts can prepare the way for greater achievements.

Every church that really has a mission in its community can have a sense of success and achievement. The success may not be in those great gains in finance and membership but there can be those earlier gains in the various departments of church life. If a church really has no such opportunities, then the reason for its existence may be called in question.

A vivid sense of mission enables a group to overcome the frustrations that are occasioned by a lack of achievement. For a smaller church, the sense of mission arises out of a realization of the spiritual needs of its community, both personal and social. A sense of commission comes to a group when the people realize that they, as a group, are needed. This in turn gives a sense of urgency and the people talk about "what they ought to do." As long as they are imbued with a sense of mission they will spend little anxious thought about their status and size.

A sense of mission leads, quite naturally, to a plan of action. Action is a builder of morale. Military men have recognized this for centuries. Morale tends to be high in campaigns but it sags during periods of inactivity. The same principle operates within churches.

If activity is to build morale, however, it must be purposive and productive. It must be so constructive that it will challenge the most intelligent members. Benjamin Franklin, in his autobiography, tells of a sea captain who knew the demoralizing effects of idleness. On days when work was slack, he would have his men polish and shine the ship's anchor for want of some more purposeful activity.[8] This superfluous activity of

[8] William N. Otto, Editor, *The Autobiography of Benjamin Franklin* (Chicago: Houghton and Mifflin, 1928), pp. 182, 183.

anchor polishing may have heightened a few sailors' morale but doubtless failed with others. Activity has been thought of as an end in itself. This has happened even in churches. In some cases, there has been too much effort expended in shining ecclesiastical anchors with little improvement in morale.

Every church board might ask itself some highly pertinent questions. Are we facing realistically the morale problem of our church? Are we willing to accept ourselves as a unit of God's Kingdom and work zealously for God's glory? Do we have a well-defined sense of mission? Do we have a carefully planned program that is designed to carry out this mission?

Every pastor and lay officer might well ask himself some highly significant personal questions. Does my leadership cause people to be optimistic and enthusiastic? Under my supervision, are people creative in planning their work? Do they obtain a sense of recognition from me as they achieve results? Do they find their association with me an inspiring and challenging experience? Do I find it easy to accept and work with people because I understand the dynamics back of their behavior? Pastors and church officers who can answer these questions in the affirmative are morale builders.

5 Planning for Action

The hit-and-miss programs of many churches give point to the observation of an astute business man who said that he had found a new reason for believing in the church as a divine institution. "No other enterprise," he said, "could survive if managed so haphazardly." This observation is uniquely relevant to smaller churches. Many of them have remained small because of hastily envisioned and short-range plans. Hit-and-miss plans are usually the result of pastors and official members working on the basis of limited knowledge of their churches and communities.

Ministers of smaller churches frequently neglect a thorough study of their churches and communities because they anticipate subtly that their pastorates may be short. They hopefully look beyond the little church to larger fields as athletic teams sometimes look beyond an unimportant game to "the big one." Again, pastors of smaller churches often do not carry on careful studies of church and community with their people because they are busy with a multitude of tasks, lacking professional and capable lay volunteers.

The official members of smaller religious groups are unconcerned often with adequate studies that relate to their churches. In the first place, they usually feel that they know their church and community. This knowledge is frequently peripheral and really superficial in relation to the basic conditions for a successful program. Secondly, laymen are often bound by traditional concepts. They sometimes have little interest in proved, up-to-date approaches in church programming, being unaware of how much their church is below modern standards of church effectiveness. Third, sometimes people in little churches, as well as in large ones, are adjusted to mediocrity, and thus have little motivation to go on with important studies and surveys.

Appraising Resources

Socrates' dictum, "Know thyself," is as applicable to institutions as to individuals, and perhaps as difficult to follow. An institution cannot prosper without a basic knowledge of its resources and limitations any more than a person can live effectively without a fair degree of self-understanding. Business places have demonstrated the values of self-understanding by their annual inventories and audits. Inventories of physical and spiritual assets are no less important to churches.

"Well begun, half done," is a maxim that applies to the work of religious institutions. At the beginning of a pastor's ministry in a church, and at other periods, he and his official members should join in appraising the resources and liabilities of their church. The appraisal should be made in four areas: (1) the adequacy and condition of buildings, grounds and equipment; (2) the financial potential of the congregation; (3) resources of leadership and service talents; and, (4) spiritual assets.

First, it is very important in today's religious world that churches face realistically the adequacy and condition of their buildings and equipment. The day is past in most communities when God's work can be advanced in a little one-room building that is in a bad condition of repair. The principle that governs this matter is that the church and its furnishings and equipment must be representative of the homes and other buildings in the community.

Every little church that is financially pressed faces a hazard at this point. Pastors and people adjust unconsciously to the run-down condition of church property. The matter of adjustment is easy, especially in situations of financial stringency. The walls of a sanctuary become smoked up so gradually that the change is almost imperceptible to the worshipers. Because of frequent use, people become accustomed to scarred church furniture and worn carpets. Poorly maintained church grounds sometimes come to be accepted as a norm by people in little congregations that are without regular janitor service. The lack of equipment is often accepted by the little church on the assumption that nothing can be done about it.

The alert pastor and his official members survey the physical needs of the church, and they propose improvements. The projects are often accepted by the congregation as a whole with enthusiasm if presented well. At other times smaller organizations within the church accept projects when they are presented clearly and a plan of action is proposed. If the congregation and all of its organizations are so lethargic that there is no response to urgent appeals for church improvement, e. g., the painting of a weather-beaten meeting house, then the most evangelistic act a pastor can perform is to get a ladder and paint brush and lead the way. As noted earlier, there is morale-building value in needed church improvement projects. A new coat of paint on a church's weather-beaten surface has given some groups revived courage and enthusiasm.

Secondly, pastors and finance committees should survey the financial resources of their congregations. The financial resources of a local church can be determined by adding the approximate incomes of all the people of the congregation. This is an easy matter in most smaller groups because the members of the finance committee usually know the general financial status of the families. In cases where the finance committee cannot postulate the incomes of the people, a check sheet listing levels of income may be distributed and the people can mark anonymously their income brackets and return the check sheet to the chairman of the committee.

The financial resources of the church should be computed on the basis of the tithe of the aggregate incomes of the people. Official committees are often amazed at the actual potential of wealth of the church when this procedure is followed. Rockwell Smith states that one church believed it was doing well to raise a budget of $5,000 per year. A survey showed that the budget would have been more than $34,000 if the people had tithed their incomes.[1]

Churches must know their financial resources in order to plan their programs with intelligence. Lack of knowledge along this line usually results in deferred opportunities and meager plans of action. Like some people, many congregations feel that they are poorer than they are.

Thirdly, the lay leadership and service resources must be surveyed if the church is to use its laymen effectively. There are three methods of making such surveys in little churches. The pastor and his official members can list many of the talents and interests of the people as they consider each name in a committee meeting. When this method is used, as with the other methods, cards are prepared for each member and placed in a file accessible to the church workers. In many churches, however, a more comprehensive talent survey should be made. Some pastors, especially upon starting the work in a new pastorate, make it a point in their pastoral calling to list the interests and talents of their people. This method serves also as a challenge to the parishioners to accept responsibilities in the church. Finally, other pastors use schedule sheets and all members and participants are asked to fill out these indicating their service interests and abilities. These sheets may be filled out actually in a public service or, better still, answered at home and returned to the church.

Fourth, the pastor must appraise the spiritual resources of his congregation. This is very important because a church's

---

[1] *Rural Church Administration* (Nashville: Abingdon-Cokesbury, 1953), p. 61.

primary reason for existence is to exert a spiritual influence in its community. If a congregation's spiritual capital is low it is unprepared to be a genuine redemptive power and it becomes only one more social institution. The pastor uses many means, some of them highly introspective, to arrive at his estimate of the level of the spiritual life that exists among his people.

In appraising the quality of Christian life in their groups pastors, especially of the smaller congregations, should be alert to the fact that spiritual life is expressed in introvertive and extrovertive types. This fact makes spiritual living rather difficult to appraise. It also has great significance in the outreach possibilities of the congregation. Churches that are introvertive often have little influence in their communities. But on the other hand, dominantly extrovertive types often lack Christian depth. Both qualities should be found in Christian groups. Genuine Christian living, in persons and groups, has both divine and human elements. There must be divine upreach and human outreach.

The pastor's primary task in preaching, and perhaps in pastoral calling, is defined in situations where the spiritual life is low or recessive. He must lead the people to effective spiritual levels. This cannot be done narrowly with only a revivalistic type of preaching composed largely of rigorous denunciations of backsliding, spiritual lethargy and spiritual timidity. There must be also constructive elements in order to strengthen the spiritual life of a lethargic or timid congregation. Positive Biblical preaching with an emphasis on spiritual resources is an important means. Bible study in small groups is also helpful. Pastoral calling with emphasis on personal devotion and victorious Christian living does much to strengthen the Christian lives of parishioners.

Surveying Community Needs and Opportunities

It is axiomatic to say that every institution must know the needs and opportunities of its community if it is to serve intelligently. Many churches, often smaller, respond with an overly simplified answer to this matter by saying that their communities need the gospel of Christ. This answer is preeminently true, of course, but some of these churches have been proclaiming the gospel for years to little groups of pious people hidden away in little meeting places. Every pastor must recognize that the personal needs of people become the unique opportunities for Christians to demonstrate vividly and proclaim powerfully the gospel. If a church is to have these opportunities it must survey its community for general and personal needs.

The first step in undertaking to accomplish this end is to determine the boundaries of the church community. The surrounding area is the church's field of service and it is as important that it know the boundaries of "its field" as it is for the farmer to know about his line fences. This is true especially in rural churches. The church area is sometimes difficult for village and country churches to determine. Communities are somewhat more easily determined in cities because main streets and boulevards often indicate the boundaries of a church's primary area.

The best way to define the limits of a church community, particularly in rural areas, is by the use of a plat map. The map of the country area should be sufficiently large to note the location of individual families. This means that two miles to an inch is a good scale for a farming area. Maps for villages and cities, of course, must have larger scales. In rural areas, including both countryside and villages under 2500 population, these maps may be obtained from a variety of places including the county agent, the county assessor's office, and the county and state highway departments. Mayors and assessors often have maps of incorporated villages. Maps of cities can be bought readily at many places including the city and county planning commissions, city and county engineers offices, and, sometimes, at stationery stores.

In the rural communities the maps are usually for townships and they show the location of every farm. Pastors should take these maps to the village banker, school superintendent and a few representative merchants and ask each to mark the limits of the community or the patronizing area, so far as his patrons are concerned. The boundaries of the community may then be drawn to include the village and all of the countryside that makes that village a center for trade, services, and education.

The second step for a pastor to take in getting a systematic understanding of his community is to study the characteristics of the population. The wise pastor learns about the racial aspects of the people. He studies the age composition of the population noting the relative percentages of children, young people, middle aged and older people so as to know the relative opportunities for service with the various ages. He notes the gains or loss in population during the last decade. He observes whether the population is stable or unstable. The wise pastor learns about the economic characteristics of the community and he acquaints himself with the working habits of the people. The United States government volume, *Population, General Characteristics,* provides much valuable information about the population of most American communities. The volume is available usually in public libraries and in college and university libraries. It can be consulted with profit by most pastors.

The third step the pastor and his church takes to get an understanding of community needs and opportunities is a community canvass. This is a house-to-house survey that is sometimes carried on by a single church and at other times, when possible, in cooperation with other churches. Specific information concerning methods and materials are available at the denominational departments of evangelism.

Teams of laymen usually carry on the house-to-house canvass after the pastor has given instructions to them. If laymen are not available for this work in the smallest churches then the pastor can go ahead with it himself. As a matter of fact, some pastors prefer to carry on personally an informal survey of their communities in the early weeks of a pastorate. They go from home to home making short get-acquainted visits. In rural areas they are usually invited into the homes upon introducing themselves. During their visits, friendly in nature, they ask about the religious interests and affiliations of the family. This information is recorded on survey cards and filed for future use. In smaller communities this method works well for most of the people are delighted to meet the new pastor that serves in their area.

The community canvass, whether carried on by laymen or pastor, is invaluable in discovering needs and opportunities. For one thing, it assists in building a prospect or responsibility list. In today's religious world a responsibility list is a *must* if a church is to grow. Without an up-to-date list of prospects a church is like a hunter who shoots without aim vainly hoping to bag some game.

There are few activities that are as effective as the community canvass in discovering specific needs and opportunities. A well conducted canvass always discovers people who are without a religious ministry. These persons are usually among the poorer people because at the present time in America most of the middle and upper class people are affiliated with a church, sometimes rather tenuously.

The discovery of religiously disenfranchised persons of the community should be accepted as an opportunity and a challenge by smaller churches. These churches should minister effectively to the poorer people who have been overlooked by the large congregations. The opportunity, however, is not always accepted by the smaller groups because many of them are also highly self-conscious about the social status of their adherents.

Several recent studies have indicated that large numbers of poorer people are neglected by all the churches of communities.

In a thorough sociological study, A. B. Hollingshead found that in a thriving midwest community ninety percent of the mothers and ninety-eight percent of the fathers of the poorest class (class V, the lower-lower class) were unknown by any local pastor or known not to attend church.[2] Harold Kaufman found that in a rural community in New York state 78% of the people in the higher prestige classes were active church members but only one percent of the people in the lower prestige classes were active in churches.[3]

Smaller churches should know who are the religiously neglected people of their communities. They should then have the Christian commitment to minister to them. They will usually have that field without competition. The acceptance of this opportunity fulfills the great commission and offers a promising field of growth to the little church.

Setting Goals

Bishop Fred Corson, of the Methodist Church, says that many congregations would double their effectiveness if they would set goals and strive to reach them. He believes that one-half of the local churches of America hardly know why they exist.[4] These churches occupy themselves with a number of routine activities without imagination and inspiration. Little is achieved because little is envisioned.

Lowell's words concerning persons are equally true of institutions, "not failure, but low aim is sin." Perhaps a greater sin than low aim is no aim. T. T. Munger is quoted as saying, "Providence has nothing good or high in store for one who does not resolutely aim at something high or good. A purpose is the eternal condition of success."

---

[2] *Elmtown's Youth* (New York: John Wiley and Sons, 1949), p. 460.

[3] *Prestige Classes in a New York Rural Community* (Ithaca, N. Y.: Cornell University, 1943), p. 16. Several years ago Liston Pope showed the class consciousness of churches in a Southern milling city.

[4] Andrew W. Blackwood, *Pastoral Leadership* (Nashville: Abingdon-Cokesbury, 1949), p. 15.

Goals are as important in the work of the church as in the life of a person. Persons of great achievement clearly envision objectives while the drifters live without worthy aims. Studies of would-be suicides show that these persons find life intolerable because they find no real purpose in it. This has happened sometimes in church life. The people have found the church dull and monotonous, and sometimes intolerable, because it envisions no great need and undertakes no great task.

A congregation without specific goals may be compared to an apathetic football team engaged in a "game" on a field without goal lines. The players are content to kick and pass the ball but no one tries to score. If one were to cross the line where the goal ought to be no one would be sufficiently interested to record the points.

Goals serve two important functions in local churches. In the first place, they give direction to the activities. They help all of the people to pull in the same direction. H. B. Trecker says that "Objectives are like maps. They show us where we want to go and point out some of the roads we may take to get there."[5] Secondly, goals help to motivate the people of a local church in their Christian activities. They help to give the people "a consciousness of what they ought to do." Goal setting has been used successfully by business concerns, both large and small. Definitely announced aims have aroused enthusiasm and stimulated activity. Local churches have realized the same results by adopting goals in their work.

Local congregations should have both quantitative and qualitative goals. Ideally, these aims extend into every important area of the congregation's life including worship, Christian nurture, social activities, and evangelism. The quantitative goals are concerned with attendance, membership and finance while the qualitative goals are related to the quality of the program.

[5] *Group Process in Administration* (New York: Woman's Press, 1950) Second Edition. p. 74.

Many churches set goals for numerical gains. This often stimulates interest and activity. A goal of ten per cent increase in Sunday school attendance within a specified period has often been the spark that got people working. The same effect has often been realized in church attendance. Likewise projected gains in church membership and finance have sometimes kindled the imagination and enthusiasm of the parishioners. Well-framed and well-publicized goals, along with intelligent action, sometimes gets a church off dead center and on the way to successful achievement.

Simple goals for numerical gains, however, may be superficial and represent the wishful thinking of a lethargic minister and congregation. If the announcement of goals is not followed by careful planning and diligent effort the congregation may be harmed. If significant achievements are not realized the congregation is likely to experience a psychological sag and be worse off than it was before the goals were announced.

If quantitative goals alone are used there are likely to be few permanent numerical gains because no adequate basis had been laid for an advance. When numerical gains are realized without a better quality of service they are likely to be superficial and short lived. Little abiding worth is realized when goals are attained only on the basis of cheap and high pressure methods.

The qualitative goals are less vivid but more basic in the life of a church. An objective to increase the effectiveness of the church school through a carefully planned leadership training program is more significant than a goal of ten per cent increase in attendance. Likewise the goal to broaden and enrich the young people's activities so that more youth may be reached for Christ will probably bring about more significant results than a short time intensive drive for increased attendance or membership. An aim to see family worship established in every church home may have greater spiritual significance than an increase in attendance at the regular services. A goal of reaching every unchurched home in the community with the gospel by lay visitation is more significant than a contest between departments in an effort to increase church attendance.

There are some important and basic criteria for the setting of successful goals. For one thing the objectives should be worked out by the group as a whole. For instance, the official board should envision the goals that relate to worship and the church school board should establish the aims that relate to the Christian education program. A great deal of motivation and enthusiasm are realized by the lay workers as they envision the aims for which they will strive. Having helped to formulate these objectives and having subscribed to them, the workers feel a sense of responsibility in helping to see that they are realized. The ambitious goals of an enterprising pastor are seldom effective when they are handed down to the people as assignments. Secondly, the objectives should be stated specifically and vividly. They need to be announced and publicized frequently in challenging terms so that people continue to be guided and motivated. Thirdly, goals should be reasonable. If the objectives are too high the people develop a sense of failure and frustration. However, if the objectives are too low they are meaningless. Finally, it is ordinarily better to have goals that lend themselves to periodical check ups. It is very important that the pastor and people know clearly the progress that is being made.

Goals become a *guiding* image to local churches when they are formulated, on the one hand, in reference to the church's resources and, on the other hand, in reference to the needs and opportunities of the community. The concept of the *guiding image* is derived from the German word, *Bestimmung,* which suggests the vivid master sentiments and motives of persons and institutions. The concept includes also a vision of what can be accomplished. There are hundreds of local churches that need nothing more than a luminous *guiding* image that has the power to capture the interests and motivate the activities of the people. Realistic objectives may be the first step toward progress.

6

Training
the
Workers

Jesus made the matter of training a small group of disciples the primary task of his ministry. He did this deliberately at the cost of being unable to give his personal attention to the multitudes who hung on his words. Unlike many modern ministers, he did not turn to the few because he could not get a large hearing. He knew that a few men who had grasped thoroughly his spirit could accomplish more than multitudes of casual followers. Had Jesus not trained these men it is likely that the Christian movement would have exhausted its energies within a generation or two.

Jesus made a twofold emphasis in the training of his disciples. In the first place he gave them systematic instruction in the principles of effective service (Matthew 10:1-15; Luke 10: 1-16). Secondly, he supervised their activities as they sought to apply these principles. He sent them out on missionary tours with instructions and upon their return he discussed their experiences with them (Luke 10:17-20). Today this method is known as in-service training and educators are rediscovering its values. Professional schools, including medical colleges and seminaries, are joining systematic instruction with supervised practice of the work the students are to do. The actual practice implements the principles that have been taught.

The importance of training lay workers is as enduring as the Christian church. The pattern of Jesus' ministry has principles that can never be outlived. These principles are as lasting as the great spiritual truths that he spoke. The present day pastor has no task that is more important than that of enlisting, training and supervising his laymen in Christian service. He can extend his influence beyond his tenure in a church by training workers who will continue to serve effectively after he has moved to another place. It is better to put ten men to work than to do the work of ten men.

The matter of training a corps of workers is uniquely important in smaller churches. These churches lack trained workers more than the large congregations. Furthermore, a little church cannot hope to have capable lay service unless it gives special attention to leadership or service training. The ultimate success or failure of every pastor's ministry depends heavily upon his success or failure in this endeavor.

A New Day for Laymen

A new day has dawned for laymen. This new day is occasioned by an awakened interest on the part of the church in lay Christian service. The awakened interest has come at a most appropriate time, for laymen now face the prospect of having more leisure time from their occupations than ever before. The new day that offers increased service opportunities to laymen also means a new day to churches.

Never before in history has the church had such a tremendous potential of lay service. Lay people have more time now for Christian service because it takes less time to make a living than formerly. In the future there will be still more lay time for Christian work. Many economists believe that in a few years millions of workers will be on a thirty hour week. The potential for the church in this situation is staggering. The church can accomplish more than ever before if it capitalizes on the services of its members.

Laymen are looking to the church for guidance in the matter of using profitably a portion of their leisure time. Consecrated Christians do not wish to spend all of their hours of leisure in holding a rod waiting for a reluctant fish to nibble on artificial bait, or in trying to put a little white ball in a hole that is a little larger than itself.

The church, like a conquering army, has no place for loafers. The demands of the Kingdom are so urgent today that every man must find his place of duty. Like an army, Christian victories are not won by officers alone but by the services of all the people in the ranks. If smaller churches are to approximate the level of effectiveness they should have, they must organize plans to train all of their members for successful Christian service.

Perhaps the local churches in the Southern Baptist Convention have given more attention to training their members generally for Christian life and service than have congregations in other denominations. The training has been carried on through the Baptist Training Union which is the counterpart of the Sunday school. The training is graded and classes are available to all ages. The classes meet normally on Sunday evening before the regular Sunday night service. There is a wide range of general courses available including studies in home missions, foreign missions, Bible, Christian doctrine, history, the church, the home, stewardship, soul-winning, and the denomination. In addition there are many courses on methods of church work including church school teaching, sacred music, the conduct of worship, missionary methods, and personal evangelism.

Hundreds of smaller congregations with regular Sunday evening meetings can profit greatly by instituting a regular study plan in an early Sunday evening service. Most congregations have youth services at that time. Let these churches organize groups of people of all ages in an early meeting. The whole family may go to the church together and each find an interest in his age group.

Enlisting Workers

Like Banquo's ghost, the problem of a limited number of lay workers haunts every smaller church. This problem, like a spectre, attends every board meeting and shows up at most of the public services. It dogs the pastor's tracks and often makes his work appear futile because of the enormity of the task with the limited number of lay workers. It is no wonder that many pastors consider this as one of their most obstinate problems. Upon closer examination, however, this problem is partly phantom and unreal. It is exaggerated often because of two false assumptions.

The first false assumption is that *there is actually little leadership potential in the church.* The problem of limited workers in a local church frequently seems greater than it is because no survey of lay interests and talents has been taken. Such surveys often turn up valuable data especially at the beginning of a pastor's ministry in a church. These surveys help encourage lay participation as well as indicate available workers. Moreover, the problem of limited workers often seems greater than it really is because of a failure to analyze the specific tasks of the church. For instance, no one ever asked, "What are the specific duties of this job, and what qualifications can fulfill its demands?" This is known as job analysis in business and it is standard procedure in the commercial and professional world. Pastors and church officials have the tendency to think in stereotypes. They sometimes approach this matter in terms of unanalyzed traditional concepts as to what the job involves. At other times they think in terms of what the last office holder was like. Finally, the problem of limited workers is frequently exaggerated because of an overly high idealism on the part of the pastor and his official members. It is sometimes assumed that unusual qualities or certain degrees of formal education are necessary for lay service. These have their value, of course, but it must be remembered that the Kingdom of God has been advanced largely by ordinary men and women. The men of the original group of apostles were not outstanding upon their appointment to work with Jesus. No one of them was formally trained. The Kingdom would have languished long ago if God had depended alone on the college bred to do his work. People of good intelligence, a love for others, and a genuine commitment to Christ have the basic qualifications to work for Christ.

There are few local churches in America that do not have a sufficient potential in their members to carry on an effective Christian program. This observation is based on the principle that every group contains within its membership enough native ability to carry on its work successfully.[1] Moreover, the fact of individual differences in people means that there is in every group a variety of potential abilities to care for many different kinds of work. These principles apply to all situations with the possible exception of groups that are extraordinarily tiny and those from which many of the young people have migrated.

The second false assumption is that *most people do not wish to serve actively in the church.* This assumption seems, at first sight, to be well founded in view of the fact that most of the lay service in American Protestantism is performed by ten per cent of the members. What about the ninety per cent? Are all of them unconcerned?

The facts are that many of the people in the latter group are ambivalent about Christian work. On the one hand they want to be active but, on the other hand, they are occupied with many other activities or are fearful to start doing regular Christian service. Large numbers of these laymen have repressed their desire to be active in Christian service because of feelings of inadequacy. They need someone to challenge them to accept assignments in the church. Furthermore, they need to be assured that proper leadership guidance and training will be provided them. Enlistment and training for leadership go hand in hand.

In the matter of enlisting workers every pastor should assume that there is a twofold basis for the latent desire of people to do Christian work. First, genuine Christians wish to serve because of their love for Christ and their concern for people.

---

[1] Harry C. Munro, "Can Laymen Teach Religion?" *International Journal of Religious Education,* 47 (May, 1952), p. 4.

It is as natural for a Christian to want to serve Christ actively as it is for a child to want to walk. Secondly, there is a deeply rooted desire in human nature to achieve something worthwhile. It is normal for Christians to wish to satisfy this deeply rooted impulse in Christian activity.

Modern life has robbed people of many of the opportunities to attain a sense of achievement. This is true in vocational, recreational, and social life. Industrialized work, commercialized entertainment, and artificial culture have left millions of people with little chance to live with a sense of doing something that is really significant. There is little sense of accomplishment, for example, in a man putting a nut on a certain bolt on a car chassis that goes by him on the belt line. In the area of recreation, for instance, it is a thrill to some people to see a halfback of their home team run eighty yards for a touchdown but the back's achievement hardly satisfies their own personal desires to do something worthwhile. Our dependence on manufactured products diminishes our opportunities for personal creativity and achievement. The nineteenth-century woman doubtless got a greater sense of accomplishment when admiring friends complimented her dress as her own creation than the twentieth-century woman gets when friends ask, "Where did you buy that beautiful dress?" The church has a responsibility to give people opportunities to satisfy their "wish to achieve." Many people volunteer for service when opportunities are presented, for they represent a chance for them to meet one of their most deeply felt needs. Others must be urged to take up Christian service with its promise to fulfill latent wishes to do something that is worthwhile.

The method of recruiting workers is important. Many smaller churches recruit these people in a casual manner by electing them by popular vote, often without nomination, in a board meeting. In cases of popular voting, officers are usually returned to their positions unless they refuse vehemently to continue their work or unless old age keeps them away from the church. A person's reelection is frequently a vote of thanks for past service. When vacancies occur someone is elected often who is noticeably available, and the most qualified people are overloaded. Every small church should insist that its pastor and a few lay members constitute a personnel committee. This committee should give much thought in discussing the kind of workers needed and it should challenge potential workers. The personnel committee also makes nominations at the annual election meetings, and at other times when vacancies occur.

The pastor's faith in his people is a basic element in his work in the personnel committee and in the whole matter of recruiting workers. It is as important for the pastor to have confidence in his people as it is for parents to believe in their children. As in the family situation, the pastor's confidence helps him see the potential for service that there is in his laymen. It furthermore inspires them to accept the church's challenge to service because he believes that they can do a task.

Training Workers

"Dedicated ignorance, or consecrated incompetence, is not very useful in the Lord's work."[2] God needs more than mere goodness to advance his work. This means that guidance and training must follow the enlistment of workers.

The local church has no single problem that is more important than the training of its lay workers. A survey of a group of pastors of smaller churches in Ohio showed that this was one of the big problems in small-church administration. In a recent study of religious education the following question was asked of a large number of ministers of churches of all sizes: "When you think of Christian education, what are the things that bother you most?" Overwhelmingly the ministers answered: "Inadequate leadership."[3] In speaking of Christian

---

[2] *Ibid.*, p. 5.

[3] John L. Lobingier, *The Better Church School* (Boston: Pilgrim Press, 1952), p. 89.

education Lobingier says, "The training of volunteer leaders is the most crucial question which Christian education faces, and upon our success in this effort—more than upon any other one factor—depends the success of our religious education program." [4] Trained lay leadership is the key that unlocks doors to success in a local church program.

The training of workers in churches today is more important than formerly because of the professional competence in public education and other community organizations. If the disparity in the quality of leadership between the church and other organizations is marked, younger people lose interest and confidence in the church.

Furthermore, training of workers is uniquely important in smaller churches. In the first place, the little churches must carry on all of their work by lay volunteer help excepting that of the pastor. They cannot afford, quite naturally, a ministerial staff. Secondly, the smaller congregation makes its appeal to its constituency and community on the basis of the quality of its leadership. It cannot attract people by its community status, social recognition, or celebrated minister. Furthermore, smaller churches, especially those that are young, have fewer professional people than the larger and older congregations. This means that more people without professional training must be trained for effective service.

The assumption that smaller churches can get along with an inferior quality of leadership is false. Many little churches have met with defeat because they made this assumption. The quality of leadership in the Kingdom cannot be graded naively on the basis of church size. In some ways a smaller church needs a higher type of leadership than large congregations.

Every smaller church can have an effective plan of leadership education. There are six types of training that are practicable for even the tiny congregations.

---

[4] *Ibid.*, p. 89.

Leadership training classes. Leadership or service training courses are offered in two ways. First, churches often cooperate in setting up these courses. Sometimes, all the churches in a community unite in organizing a training school at a central place. At other times the churches of a single denomination set up a leadership education school. Secondly, local churches provide their own leadership training courses. Ideally churches should participate in both of these plans if cooperative schools are available.

There is a wide variety of ways in which a local church can offer service training courses to its own group. Perhaps the most usual way is to have a training class on one night a week for five or ten successive weeks. Such a course is often held in the fall or at the beginning of the church year. Sometimes, however, these courses are offered during Lent when special attention is given to studies that deal with the life of Christ and the gospels. At other times courses are given on five successive nights of a single week, perhaps at the beginning of the church year. Other pastors have offered courses dealing with Biblical studies in connection with their prayer meetings. This occasions lengthening the prayer service so that time for study will be allowed. Other churches have used these courses effectively in early Sunday evening meetings. Furthermore, an increasingly large number of congregations are offering leadership training courses in their Sunday schools. A leadership training class is organized and attended by people who anticipate Christian service. Sometimes such a course is offered each year to the young people's class upon the assumption that all Christian youth should know basic principles of Christian leadership.

Workers' conferences. The workers' conference offers a uniquely fine opportunity for leadership training. Its genius lies in the fact that its interest is focused in the specific purposes and problems of the local church. Within that context principles and methods of Christian service are studied. New materials are discussed. Audio-visual aids are demonstrated.

Frequently, little churches have a modified type of workers' conference by making a study session the top priority in the monthly board meetings. Immediately after devotions a serious study is conducted on church school methods or Biblical teachings. The study often follows the outline of a basic textbook. Business matters follow the study period and the session is concluded with fellowship. One little church doubled its membership in a year's time by following this method.

In addition to giving information, the workers' conference is an important agency in building an *esprit de corps* among the members. The people come to feel that they are a team as they discuss their problems together.

Directed Readings. The workers' conference can accomplish a great deal by carrying on a plan of directed reading among its members. In such a plan there is a reading club promoter or secretary who introduces new books and magazine articles. The secretary of reading promotes by every means the reading of books. In some cases certificates for reading are awarded.

This plan relates closely to a workers' library. If a library is already established in the church the reading secretary publicizes good books in Christian education. If there is no library, or no shelf of books for church workers, one should be started and the books should be circulated. Even $25.00 makes a start for a workers' shelf of books for the small church. This small beginning should then be augmented by additions from month to month.

Correspondence Courses. Correspondence courses are uniquely appropriate to churches that cannot carry on a strong program of leadership education classes. These courses can be done by anyone on the basis of his own time schedule. Unusual values are realized by those who apply themselves. Many of the denominations have a fine selection of correspondence courses. The leadership training departments of all denominations can give information about them.

Assistants. Many churches are carrying on effective leadership training through a plan of assistant church officers and Sunday school teachers. Assistants differ from substitutes, e.g., substitute teachers, in that the former maintain a continual relationship with the regular officer or teacher, helping in every aspect of the work. The plan of assistant teachers is particularly helpful to small churches with a limited number of mature and capable workers. It enables qualified teachers to conduct larger classes because of the assistance of a helper.

The assistant teacher or officer, often a younger person, finds his experience a valuable apprenticeship. He helps plan the work, he sees principles of effective service demonstrated and he actually shares in the process himself. He assumes the responsibilities of the work in the occasional absence of the regular teacher or officer.

Coaching and Supervision. The matter of personal coaching and supervision is an important supplement to other forms of leadership education in the smaller church. Frequently the pastor has the chief responsibility in this matter. He makes the matter of counseling with his church workers a primary concern. He discusses their problems of lay service in his regular pastoral calls. The pastor does not teach a Sunday school class but he visits every department and class as a friendly counselor. His work in coaching and supervision is supplemented, of course, by the work of the Sunday school superintendent, department superintendents, and other capable church officers.

Some churches have found it valuable to call in specialists in religious education for daily vacation Bible schools and series of children's evangelistic meetings. Not only do these trained educators head up the Bible school or special meeting but they seek to demonstrate to the workers the principles of effective service. As time permits, they counsel all the workers on their problems. They sometimes give systematic instruction in effective church school work. This plan unites the values of a successful Bible school or other special meeting with capable instruction in Christian service.

The basic problem in many smaller churches is to create the desire on the part of the workers for leadership training. In some cases, the workers are unaware of the standards of effective lay service and they thus see little need for training. In other cases, people, being overly conservative, idealize the former ways of doing things. They have not realized that the prophetic injunction, "ask for the old ways and walk in them," was not spoken to discourage creative methodology but that it rather referred to eternal principles of righteousness. Smaller churches, as smaller groups generally, tend to be more conservative in methodology than larger churches.

The wise pastor helps to create a consciousness of efficiency among his church workers in order to overcome the nonchalant attitudes about training. He refers frequently to effective Christian service in his sermons. He discusses the principles of successful church work in addresses to the various groups. He encourages efficient approaches to various problems in board meetings. He encourages every suitable type of leadership training for his church. He talks about working effectively for Christ in his pastoral calling and other personal interviews.

Obvious need for leadership classes + more Bible study

7 Organizing for Action

Russell R. Patton, pastor of the Epworth Methodist Church, Lexington, Kentucky, says that when people move into a community they frequently decide which church to attend on the basis of what the church can offer the members of their families. In visiting the churches of the community these people ask a number of pertinent questions: "How good is the Sunday school?" "Does the church have a nursery?" "What boys' and girls' clubs does it have?" "What adult activities does it sponsor?" and "What about the quality of its music?" These questions underscore the necessity for churches to have well-organized programs under the direction of capable leaders.

The smaller church faces one of its most difficult problems in the matter of having a well organized program. In the first place, it frequently confronts apathetic attitudes on the part of many of its members toward effective organizations. It also encounters the problems that arise out of the lack of trained personnel and sufficient finance. These problems must be solved, however, because the day is past when a church can prosper with a simple program consisting of a Sunday school, two weekly preaching services, a prayer meeting, and a modicum of pastoral calling.

Many of the smaller churches have been slow to realize the importance of church organization because of certain traditions in American Protestantism. These traditions arose out of the early patterns of the circuit ministry. In the frontier days smaller churches were usually joined together in large circuits. Many of the smaller churches were visited by their pastors only once or twice a month. The pastor preached for the congregation and moved on to other points. There was a meager type of pastoral care and little attention was given to church organization. As a matter of fact, there were few well defined areas of service available to laymen. Sunday schools were unknown in the colonial days and little attention was given to youth work or specified children's activities. American Protestantism arose in a preaching tradition as indicated by the fact that clergymen were popularly called preachers instead of pastors or ministers.

Moreover, some contemporary pastors fail to properly organize their churches because of a misunderstanding of the necessity of the divine-human cooperation in building the Kingdom of God. They overly depend on God in relation to their own efforts. This attitude is sometimes expressed in ministers' meetings, "What we need is the power of God and not human efforts and plans." While it must be recognized that God's power is basic in building the Kingdom, such an attitude often represents an escape mechanism from the hard work of planning and supervising the activities of the church. For instance, prayer often becomes a retreat from work. I have heard devout people pray fervently in the midweek prayer meeting that God would "send sinners to our meetings" while they did nothing to invite them to come. There are hundreds of churches in which people pray earnestly that God will give them a great revival and "a rich harvest of souls" but many of these churches have never organized a group of lay evangelistic visitors. Such churches are presuming upon God.

E. P. Boyd, once a pastor in a small town in southern Illinois, reported a vivid account of how devout people substituted prayer for organization and action. A splendid Christian man, member of a small church, had been nominated for mayor in the little town in which Boyd lived. The other nominee for mayor was a man of low character, lacking principles of civic righteousness. The people of the little church spent much time in prayer prior to election day. They earnestly prayed that the cause of righteousness would win, but they made no organized efforts to get out the vote of the people who favored civic righteousness. On election day these church folks prayed so fervently that they themselves neglected to go to the polls. Their candidate lost the election by a few votes.

Setting Up An Organization

The smaller church confronts one of its most difficult problems at the point of setting up a program that is adequately organized so that it can meet the needs of its congregation and appeal to others. A large number of the smaller churches fail here. On the basis of adequacy there are three types of church organization. These types range from the barely organized to those that are set up in an effective manner.

First, there are those churches that are organized to provide only preaching, pastoral calling, and perfunctory Sunday school work. This type is a survival of a former generation, as noted above, and it is found most frequently in circuits where churches receive only part-time ministerial service. This type of organization, however, is sometimes found in churches that have resident pastors. In such cases, pastors and people lack organizational imagination and genius. Few results can be anticipated from such a barren church program because the lines of outreach into the community are too limited.

Secondly, many churches are organized in accordance with their denominational disciplines or manuals, having the regular offices and functions that are prescribed by headquarters. Children's and youth activities, for instance, are organized properly after the denominational pattern. Interests such as missions and stewardship have been cared for by the election of officers and committees.

This type of organization is good as far as it goes. Quite

naturally, local churches should follow the denominational patterns for organization but if they do that only, their organizational set-up lacks imagination and adaptation to their unique situations. Such a program makes a church an organization only and not an organism with its own individualistic life. Organization by prescription only contributes to the maintenance of the *status quo*.

Thirdly, there is a creative type of organization that, on the one hand, fulfills all denominational requirements but, on the other hand, transcends them in imagination and adaptation to the unique needs of the congregation and community. Local congregations have accomplished this by organizing evangelistic groups to take the gospel to every unreached person in their communities. Frequently these groups have gone to religiously disenfranchised persons such as racial minorities and migrants. In industrial centers groups of laymen have organized to take the gospel to men working in shops. They have held short services at the noon hour with the consent of the management of the plant. Local churches have organized Bible classes in homes in an effort to reach children who did not attend church school.

The first major organizational task of the smaller congregation is to set up an organization that meets the needs of its own people and has an outreach to others. Ideally, its organization should be set up to meet the worship, Christian education, fellowship, and service needs of the people. Its program must recognize, of course, the various age differences of its congregation and, in so far as possible, have graded activities. This is a big order for the smaller church and there is no easy way of meeting it. Perhaps the solution is seen primarily in the congregation's recognition of the importance of this problem. When that happens most congregations start a movement to expand their programs. They are alert to recruit and train new workers to assume added responsibilities. They often demonstrate a fine genius in providing finance and equipment for the expanded program.

The second major organizational task of the church is to get a proper distribution of responsibilities among its laymen. In cases where the number of workers is limited it frequently happens that two or three persons are overworked and other people, perhaps younger and less aggressive, have little to do. I was acquainted with one congregation in which one man held three of the five major offices. This situation arises frequently because of the lack of alertness in recruiting workers. At other times, however, two other important factors are involved: (1) the "church boss," and (2) seniority rights.

Little churches are frequently dominated by a single layman, or two. This situation is so prevalent that in every seminary course in church administration some frustrated student pastor asks about what the minister can do in cases where a layman assumes a managerial relationship to the congregation. This situation is found more often in little churches than in large ones. Smaller congregations permit aggressive persons to become dominant. Sometimes the congregations are heavily dependent on the financial help of an aggressive layman. Frequently, especially in the early days of a local church, it is necessary to rely heavily on the leadership of a few laymen and it frequently happens that some of these come to feel that the local church represents one of their private enterprises.

A closely related problem grows out of the "seniority rights" of the workers. Lay workers come to feel that they have permanent tenure on their offices because they have held them for a few years. When this situation develops the workers often become routine and unimaginative in their service and the whole program is hindered.

These problems must be confronted when they exist. There are three approaches that are sometimes helpful. In the first place, let the church adopt as a working motto, "A task for every man, and a man for every task." This ideal, properly publicized, helps prepare the way for a proper distribution of responsibilities. Again, a few churches have handled these problems by limiting the tenure on some of the church offices. In some cases, for instance, no lay officer could hold a specific office for longer than three years. This method has a considerable limitation because it removes effective people who ought to continue their work as well as removing those who improperly claim seniority rights. Finally, the method of assistants is sometimes helpful in the solution of these difficulties. In some cases an assistant so distinguishes himself in his work that his election to an office filled by an incompetent person is assured.

The third major organizational task of the smaller church is to get all of the workers to accept responsibility for their offices and assignments. This is frequently difficult and reasons for it inhere in the nature of smaller congregations. Often workers feel that their work is not really important because the groups are small. At other times they lose a sense of the significance of their tasks because they are so well acquainted with the members of their groups that everything is on a free-and-easy basis. Moreover, organization in smaller churches is often casual with too little dignity put on lay offices. Frequently the church does not emphasize the importance of each task in relationship to the total program.

Churches can do a few simple things to help all of the laymen to accept responsibility for their assignments. In the first place let lay service be dignified by inaugural services for the principal officers at which time the pastors commission the workers. Again, let there be a hearty recognition of achievements so that workers have a sense of accomplishment when work has been well performed. Finally, let there be no responsibility without accountability. Reports on problems encountered and work done should be made to the committees, boards, and the pastor.

The pastor's responsibility in the organization of the church should be recognized clearly by himself and by his laymen. He is the head of the organization and his position makes him ultimately responsible for every activity. He inspires, counsels, and directs the entire organization. He is an ecclesiastical trouble shooter ready to assist when lay officers get to the end of their resources. If some department does not function well it is his responsibility to see that the problem is solved. He shares in every success and every failure of all the church organizations. Some credit is his if the Woman's Missionary Society does well. On the other hand, the ultimate failure is his if the work in the nursery department breaks down.

Planning the Work of a Circuit

Pastors of circuits encounter unique and difficult problems due to the fact that they serve in more than one community. It has been known for a long time that a multiple-church parish makes effective ministerial work very difficult, but the system is continued because there are not enough preachers for all of the churches and, furthermore, small congregations must be grouped together in order to provide a salary for the pastor. The circuit system is more general than many people realize. More than one-third of the churches of America are joined in multiple-church parishes.

There are a few unique emphases that are necessary in successful circuit work. Some of these relate to the pastor's organization of his own work program and others have to do with the organization of the churches.

First, pastors with more than one congregation are finding it helpful to schedule their time equitably, with the designation of certain days of the week for each of the churches in their circuits. The apportionment of time is made on the basis of church size, support, needs, and every other relevant factor. The observance of such a weekly schedule especially commends itself to the people living in communities most distant from the parsonage. The people at the crossroads church, for instance, become convinced that their pastor recognizes their needs and the opportunities of their congregation when he regularly spends Tuesday of each week in their community. Moreover, such a plan gives a professional standing to the pastor's work that is totally absent when he goes to the various churches on a hit-and-miss basis. Furthermore, it makes it possible for the people of all the churches and communities to know when they can contact the minister. The satisfaction of the people, particularly at the peripheral points, is reflected in an increased support of the whole church program, including the circuit budget.

The circuit pastor trains his people to take the initiative in requesting pastoral care on the days he spends in their communities. This is especially necessary in the churches that are not located near the parsonage. The pastor obviously cannot be well acquainted with all of the pastoral needs of a community in which he does not live.

Secondly, the church, or churches, at a distance from the parsonage in a circuit often appoint a layman to act as a liaison between the parishioners and the pastor. The name and functions of this layman are publicized by public announcements, bulletin boards, and by other means so that all of the people of the community may know whom to contact in case of need. This lay assistant receives calls and messages for the pastor and relays them to him. In some cases he has the personal qualifications to carry on some of the pastoral duties in the absence of the minister.

Thirdly, the circuit pastor gives major attention to the enlistment and training of laymen. This is of primary importance because he must rely more heavily on lay leadership than the pastor of a single church. It often happens, for instance, that a circuit pastor never has an opportunity to attend the Sunday schools of his church. Such a situation calls for trained and capable workers.

Moreover, the circuit pastor must sometimes depend upon laymen for leadership in public worship services, including the message. Thoughtful laymen who live a consistent Christian life and who have a sense of spiritual urgency can make a large contribution in the absence of the pastor. Elton Trueblood emphasizes that laymen actually have certain advantages over clergymen in the matter of giving religious messages. For one thing the layman's message is given without pay and some people accept his words more readily because of that fact. Moreover, Trueblood points out, laymen have an advantage because they are closer to the common life and there is a certain freshness in what they say.[1]

This type of religious address should be characterized by the unique insights that laymen have obtained from their orientation to life and to their vocation. Their messages should not be only an organized set of Christian platitudes but the Bible should be interpreted in the light of lay experience. The thoughtful school teacher, business man, and farmer often have insights into the Word, the textbook of life, that have escaped the clergymen. Circuit churches, with the pulpits occupied only a fraction of the time by their ministers, profit greatly from the public ministry of laymen. The circuit pastor has an important function in enlisting, challenging, and training lay preachers.

Fourth, the successful circuit pastor makes a generous use of the telephone and the mail service in an effort to maintain contact with all of his people in the various communities. He must frequently substitute a telephone call or a written card or note for a pastoral call because of distance and time.

The parish paper is an invaluable tool to the circuit preacher, especially if he has three or more churches. He carries many of the announcements in this paper that would be emphasized by various means were he spending all of his time in one community. A good parish paper, moreover, stimulates a hearty spirit of competition between the churches of a circuit and

---

[1] Elton Trueblood, *Your Other Vocation* (New York: Harpers, 1952), pp. 40-43.

people increase their efforts when they read about the achievements of other churches. In such an instance, the people will say, "If the folks at the crossroads church can do it, so can we." Furthermore, a parish paper integrates the congregations of a circuit. It is an effective agent in promoting union meetings and cooperative projects. Moreover, it integrates a circuit by reporting the personal news items of a parish. Everyone likes to read about his neighbors. Cooperation becomes hearty when the people become acquainted with each other.

Supervising the Work

There is a growing awareness of the importance of church administration in American Protestantism. Several years ago an important study showed that denominational leaders rated administrative gifts to be first in importance in successful pastors.[2] On the basis of a comprehensive study Samuel Blizzard reports that the average Protestant pastor spends one half of his time in organizational and administrative work. He devotes almost twice as much time in supervising the activities of the church as he spends in preparing for preaching and worship.[3] In a lighter vein, Roland Q. Leavell seeks to emphasize the contemporary importance of pastoral administration by stating, "Today it takes more technical skill to direct the 'Sunbeam Band' than it took to be the pastor of a church fifty years ago."[4]

On first thought it may be assumed that pastoral administration is much less important in a small church than in a large one. It is true that the little congregation has fewer organizations to direct but, on the other hand, it presents unique difficulties in the smallness of its numbers, the lack of its facilities, the difficulties that arise out of interpersonal relationships, and

---

[2] Cf., A. W. Beaven, *The Local Church* (Nashville: Abingdon-Cokesbury, 1937), pp. 155-156.

[3] "The Ministers' Dilemma," *The Christian Century* (April 25, 1956), p. 509.

[4] "Southern Baptist Seminaries," *The Christian Century* (April 27, 1955), p. 500.

its problems of morale. Andrew Blackwood observes, "Strange as it may seem, a small church often proves more difficult to lead than one of moderate size."[5]

Leonard Mayo says that administration is "the determination and clarification of function; the formulation of policies and procedures; the delegation of authority; the selection, supervision, and training of the staff; and the mobilization and organization of all available and appropriate resources to the end that purposes of the agency (organization) may be fulfilled."[6] H. B. Trecker says more simply that administration is "a process of working with people to set goals, to build organizational relationships, to distribute responsibility, to conduct programs, and to evaluate accomplishments."[7] Trecker emphasizes that "the real focus of administration is the relationship with and between people."[8] This is especially important in the smaller church because of the close interpersonal relationships.

There are four essential qualities that are uniquely important for effective leadership in smaller churches. First, the pastor, as leader of the church, must have the ability to envision opportunities for growth. The smaller church cannot be satisfied to hold its own. It must grow or its people will lose heart. Secondly, he must have the ability to challenge all of his people to accept responsibility in the church work. The smaller church has no place for inactive members. Thirdly, he must be able to recognize the appearance of personal tensions between people and have the ability to settle them. Finally, he must have resources of confidence, optimism, and courage in order to help maintain the morale of the people when the going is hard.

---

[5] Andrew Blackwood, *Pastoral Leadership* (Nashville: Abingdon-Cokesbury, 1949), p. 259.

[6] Leonard Mayo, "Administration of Social Agencies," *Social Work Yearbook*, 1945 (New York: Russell Sage Foundation, 1945), p. 15.

[7] H. B. Trecker, *Group Process in Administration* (New York: Woman's Press, 1950), p. 2.

[8] *Ibid.*, p. 2.

The basic task of the pastor-administrator, stated most simply, is to maintain organizational efficiency with an effective type of leadership. Every pastor faces a twofold hazard at this point. On the one hand, there is the easy going and *laissez-faire* kind of administration. Men of this type often retreat into the quiet of their studies to escape the frustrations of the practical affairs of the church. On the other hand, there are autocratic pastor-administrators. These men serve as little Protestant popes over pitifully small dioceses.

The *laissez-faire* leader takes little initiative in leading the church. He usually permits the congregation to go its own way and assists only as requested. When asked to give guidance he only reflects the thinking of his people. He is often introvertive and personally insecure.

The autocratic leader is overly dominant in his administration, often dispensing with appropriate committees. He sometimes supplants board planning with his own decisions. In board meetings he is overly aggressive and seeks rubber stamp decisions of his own conclusions. He discounts other people's ideas and discourages initiative on the part of the laymen. People in small churches resent autocratic leadership and the tenure of such pastors is usually short.

Smaller churches must have democratic leadership for effective functioning. In this type of administration the leadership resources of the whole congregation are pooled. The minister contributes his special gifts and professional training and the laymen contribute their talents and lay perspective. Such a situation provides for the optimum opportunities for obtaining ideas and for evaluating the ideas suggested.

Democratic leadership provides for the maximum of motivation in the matter of carrying out the program. The people feel personally responsible for the work because they have helped define the objectives and have assisted in the making of plans. Energies are expended generously because there is a high sense of personal interest in the work. The sense of mutuality makes the whole matter of working together a delightful experience for everyone.

Democratic leadership, moreover, helps maintain the morale of the people. Personal confidence increases as one's ideas are evaluated and, perhaps, accepted by a group. Laymen have a sense of personal worth and of being needed as they share in corporate planning. Their morale and enthusiasm for the common cause rise as they contribute ideas and efforts to the on-going of the Kingdom.

Good organization and methods provide means whereby the Holy Spirit can work. Sincere and dedicated Christians become a channel for Him when they are organized to carry out clearly envisioned tasks of Christian service. Well-planned methods become open doors through which the Spirit may enter. If a church has one organization with one method, it opens one door to the Holy Spirit. If it has ten effective organizations with ten methods, it opens ten doors to Him.

Genuine spiritual achievements are always the result of Divine-human effort. In other words, it takes both God and man to make a church prosper. Paul clearly announces this principle, "I have planted, Apollos watered; but God gave the increase" (I Corinthians 3:6). It takes effective planning along with believing prayers, the intelligence of man plus the wisdom of God, and the organized efforts of the church plus the power of the Holy Spirit.

Carrying on a Comprehensive Program

8

Every local church should earn the right to be in its community. This right can be earned only by a genuine concern for the people. The effective church must have a sincere spiritual impulse that motivates it to carry on a comprehensive program in an effort to meet the needs in the community. It must have a real compassion for the unfortunate, the poor, the sick, and the sorrowing. It must seek out the anxious and frustrated and help them by true Christian fellowship. It must care about the neighborhood boy who missed the way and it must show understanding for his family. It must be a crusading force against social evils that seek the damnation of people, especially the young. It must have a burden for the lost.

There are many smaller churches, however, that seem irrelevant in their neighborhoods because they carry on narrow and limited programs. Their main activities are public worship with an emphasis on preaching and an occasional revival meeting. It often happens, especially in cities, that only a small per cent of the members actually live in the neighborhood and the church is not cognizant of individual needs. Sometimes few children of the neighborhood attend the Sunday school.

I was recently in a small city trying to locate such a church. I inquired of a gasoline station attendant about the church's location. The attendant assured me that he had never heard of that church though he had lived in the city all his life. Upon further inquiry and search I finally found the church situated one block from the gasoline station where I first stopped. The church had no bulletin board which announced its name but, worse still, it was actually anonymous and unknown in its community.

There are hundreds of churches like that in America. They are languishing because they carry on narrow and limited programs. They have remained small because their ministry has been small. They have not reached people because they used few means of outreach. Paul's law of harvest applies to institutions as well as to individuals, "He which soweth sparingly shall reap also sparingly; and he that soweth bountifully shall reap also bountifully" (II Corinthians 9:6).

Defining the Christian Pattern

Jesus set the pattern for a comprehensive ministry. He united the evangelism of words and the evangelism of deeds. He healed the sick, fed the hungry, and helped the helpless. He not only had compassion on the poor but he organized his disciples to provide for them. He taught the uninstructed, counseled the frustrated, and comforted the sorrowing. The accounts of his personal attention to individuals in need are more extensive in the Gospels than are his public discourses. In T. R. Glover's fine phrase, "Jesus was always at leisure for individuals."[1] His ministry was as broad as human need and he had a concern for the total welfare of man.

Furthermore, the manner in which Jesus went about his ministry is really more important than the things he actually did. He maintained a common touch with man so that the poorest and the most ignorant might approach him. He was person-minded, always maintaining a cordial attitude toward the needy (John 4:7; Luke 19:1-10). Not only was he alert to human needs but he took the initiative in offering his help (John 5:6; Luke 19:1-10). He was not only available to the

---

[1] T. R. Glover, *Jesus in the Experience of Men* (New York: Doran, 1921), p. 134.

distressed but he actually looked for them. He did not wait for them to come to him; he went to them. He sought out the sinful and he made friends of publicans and sinners so that he might save them (Mark 2:13-17).

The distinguished Jewish rabbi, C. A. Montefiore, in comparing the ministry of Jesus with that of the rabbis is reported as saying, "They (the rabbis), too, welcomed the sinner in his repentance. But to *seek out* the sinner, and, instead of avoiding the bad companion, to choose him as your friend in order to work out his moral redemption, this was, I fancy, something new in the religious history of Israel." A. B. Bruce also contends that Jesus's example of loving and seeking the lost "was a new thing on the earth," the appearance of which marks a new era.[2]

The early Christians saw clearly Jesus' example of ministry and they followed it diligently. In the first place they created a new type of religious ministry in order to carry on a comprehensive service designed to meet individual needs. These ministers were called deacons and their appearance marks the beginning of an epoch in the religious ministry of the world. Before the rise of the Christian church the world had known the priesthood with its varied sacerdotal forms; prophets had appeared again and again as special messengers of God; and religious teachers had taught the disciples of the various faiths; but the world had seldom seen full-time practical workers who ministered to the physical and temporal needs of the people.

During the earliest centuries of Christian history the deacons distinguished themselves as "doers of good works, searching about everywhere day and night" in an effort to find human need and to minister to it (Apostolic Canons 6:1, 2). In a vivid and true statement, the Apostolic Constitutions refers to deacons as "the ears and eyes and mouth and heart" of the bishops (2:44). This same source calls them, in another place,

---

[2] Bruce, A. B., *The Galilean Gospel* (New York: MacMillan, 1882), p. 74.

"the soul and senses of the bishops" (3:19). Deacons of the early church were not concerned primarily with preaching or public worship because that was done chiefly by the bishops. Neither were they concerned greatly about the administration of the church inasmuch as that was cared for largely by the presbyters. These men were community workers, searching for the distressed so that they might express the church's concern for them. They testified cogently of the early Christian's concern about a comprehensive ministry designed to meet broadly the needs of men.

The early Christians did not leave all of the work of ministering to human need to the clergy. The whole church was concerned in that matter. The early believers were devoted to the care of the poor, often fasting whole days so that they might have something to share with the impoverished. The early church, ministers and laymen, organized to care systematically for widows and orphans at a time when the indigent were left to the whimsical mercies of a calloused generation. The Christians put their lives in jeopardy in taking food and medicine to prisoners languishing in jails and mines. They tenderly cared for the sick, infirm, and disabled in a generation that considered the incapacitated as a drag upon society. They courageously remained in plague-ridden cities, after all the able-bodied people had fled, tenderly caring for the stricken and respectfully burying those who had fallen dead in the streets. They treated slaves, of whom there were many, as respected brethren, helping relieve their burdens. Their compassion was as broad as human need and they were tireless in their efforts to relieve it.

The validity of Jesus' concept of a comprehensive ministry has been demonstrated graphically in the history of the church. The Puritan pastor, Richard Baxter, validated it in the seventeenth century. As a young man he went to the ecclesiastically despised parish of Kidderminster that had been served by a succession of ne'er-do-well ministers. The people in that community of about 4,000 inhabitants were ignorant, immoral, and irreverent. Baxter inaugurated immediately a comprehensive program designed to minister to the urgent needs of the people so that he might win them to Christ. He took the lead in organizing poor relief and education. He was active in the public affairs of the community ever seeking civic justice and righteousness. He personally learned the rudiments of medicine and served as a physician for a period of five or six years until a doctor could be secured. He served as counselor to all of the people on all kinds of problems.

In his work at Kidderminster, Baxter was interested in more than a social service ministry. He was desirous of the conversion and spiritual growth of the people. Being always in precarious health himself, he said that he preached as "a dying man to dying men." He instructed his converts and all the people carefully in personal conferences concerning the meaning of spiritual living. The results of his ministry were phenomenal. At the time he began his work in Kidderminster there were few devout people but by the time of his death there were eight hundred active Christian families.

Equally dramatic is the story of another of Protestant's great pastors, John Oberlin, who is remembered for his achievements through a comprehensive ministry in an impoverished district in the Vosges mountains in Alsace. Oberlin's compassion was as broad as the people's needs. When he saw an ignorant keeper of pigs undertaking to teach children in a schoolhouse that was a hovel, he crusaded for a new school with teachers trained in effective methods. He inspired the people to use better methods in agriculture when he saw that they were poor and undernourished because of slipshod methods of farming. He took the lead in getting a factory into the area for the unemployed. He encouraged the villagers and country people to build roads that were passable. He cared for the sick and encouraged young men of the area to get medical training and return to serve the people.

The people of the villages served by Oberlin became concerned with the gospel he preached because he was concerned in them. He, too, left a strong parish at the time of his death. His influence has gone around the world inspiring rural church work everywhere. Oberlin College in Ohio is named for him. The villagers of the Vosges mountains still place flowers on his grave, more than 125 years after his death, in an effort to express their appreciation for a man who really cared.

John Wesley was a man of broad human concerns in his ministry. As a young man he started a lifelong habit of calling on the sick and impoverished. He was always a champion of the poor and often took up funds for their relief. More constructively, however, he organized projects for the employment of the idle and he instituted loaning societies to lend money to the hard pressed. He was interested in the health of the people and wrote a home medical manual, *Primitive Physique,* that went through forty editions. He established schools for poor children whose parents were unable to pay for their tuition and he set up orphanages for the homeless. He crusaded for the emancipation of slaves and he worked diligently for temperance. The distinguished historian, Greene, has been quoted often as saying, "John Wesley was the greatest philanthropist and social reformer of the eighteenth century. He devoted his life to the masses for whose souls and bodies in those days no man cared. To the outcast and degraded he was a messenger of mercy." [3] Wesley's life was so filled with personal benevolent deeds that he died a poor man though he might have been rich. In old age he wrote to the Commissioners of Excise, "I have two silver spoons at London and two at Bristol. This is all the plate I have at present and I shall not buy any more while so many around me want bread." [4]

---

[3] Ralph S. Cushman, *Essential Evangelism* (Nashville: Tidings, 1946), p. 54.

[4] John W. Bready, *This Freedom Whence?"* (New York: American Tract Society, 1942), p. 139.

John Wesley led the greatest evangelistic crusade from the days of early Christianity to the present time. He established a movement that was distinguished for its profound spirituality. He knew, however, that evangelism and spiritual life could not be promoted in a narrow context. He was thus concerned with the whole of men's lives.

One of the world's greatest evangelists, George Whitefield, maintained a broad concern for man. The story of his benevolent interests in both England and America is well known. That astute observer, Benjamin Franklin, characterized his broad spirit by saying, "I knew him intimately upward of thirty years. His integrity, disinterestedness and indefatigable zeal in prosecuting every good work, I have never seen equalled, and shall never see excelled." [5]

The founders of American Methodism shared the broad spirit of Wesley and Whitefield. On the one hand, they believed that people had to be redeemed personally and that the Kingdom of God would not come with improving men's economic, political, and social environment. But, also significant, they knew that man's environment was an important factor in his salvation. The pioneer American Methodists knew that the church had to relate itself to a sinner's environment in order to save him. At the celebrated Christmas Conference in Baltimore in 1784 they declared their mission in America, "to reform the continent and to spread scriptural holiness over these lands." The Methodist church became strong under the guidance of the early Methodist preachers because they implemented that twofold principle. A contemporary Methodist, Bishop Ralph S. Cushman, says, "Without doubt the secret of the tremendous growth of the Methodist societies in the first 100 years in America lay in the fact that they kept these two great objectives together." [6] Cushman further emphasizes the contemporary

[5] Inscription on Whitefield's monument on the University of Pennsylvania campus.

[6] Op. Cit.

importance of this twofold principle, "The reformer who is not interested in the spiritual regeneration of people is just as much a nuisance as the holiness preacher who shows no concern over the moral regeneration of a community or continent." [7]

In a real sense, every minister and every local church must validate the gospel they preach by a broad ministry that demonstrates genuine concern for people. A church must manifest its own love for people if it declares that God loved the world enough to send His son to save it. A church's message is hollow without that kind of demonstration.

Demonstrating the Gospel

Every small church needs to demonstrate the gospel in a comprehensive program of loving deeds in order to redeem the word power of the gospel in its community. There is a tragic loss of word power in our generation. People have become suspicious of words, even religious words. Every preacher confronts this problem when he rises to declare the gospel and every personal worker encounters it when he witnesses for Christ.

The loss of the word power of the gospel has come about partly because words themselves have become cheap in our generation. One can buy 50,000 of them for a nickel at any news stand. Still more reasonably one can get them freely from his radio or television set. They pour out in an unending stream at the flip of a switch. Moreover, the quality of words themselves has been lowered in our generation. Words have been frequently used insincerely with the intent of concealing truth rather than revealing it. They have been used extravagantly in order to sell gadgets. The insincere and extravagant use of words, particularly in mass communication, has caused many people to be suspicious of all words. This situation is somewhat unique in our times. Before the advent of modern mass communication men lived on fewer, and perhaps more sincere,

---

[7] *Ibid.*, p. 54.

words. Previously words came primarily from family, neighbors, and trusted associates.

Even religious groups have diminished the power of their own sacred words. They have sometimes used terms equivocally, even in official statements. Some of the cults have given bizarre meanings to hallowed words, but on the other hand, some of the older denominations have so denatured holy terms that they have lost all significant religious content. Words, such as salvation, faith, repentance, and redemption, have been used so variously by different groups that they have become ambiguous to the common man. The meaning of salvation, for instance, varies from psychological adjustment, as used by some liberals, to a personal renewal by the Spirit of God. The term, God, has been used to suggest everything from a local deity presiding over a cult of heterogeneous people in Harlem to an impersonal natural force in the universe. Moreover, churches have lessened the effectiveness of their sacred words by competitive appeals for adherents. No wonder there is confusion among the unchurched when a hundred voices cry over radio and television that their movements represent the only way to God. This has convinced some people that words are used as extravagantly by churches in a type of ecclesiastical salesmanship as in any other type of promotion.

I recently visited a church that was at the point of closing though it was in a flourishing community that had many human needs. The failure of that church was not because of a lack of religious words. It had sought, quite literally, to live on words. There had been ten thousand of them spoken every Sunday. It had carried on a limited program that consisted, primarily, of the proclamation or recitation of religious words. There had been a scarcity of deeds. As suggested before, few of the members of this church lived in the community and they cared little about what happened there. As a matter of fact, little attention was given to the people who lived in the church neighborhood. The lack of interest in the community and its needs had actually caused this church to become irrelevant in its neighborhood.

We must redeem the power of gospel words by a vivid demonstration of the gospel itself. In this chapter we are primarily concerned with a demonstration of the gospel in a comprehensive pastoral program designed to meet the present as well as the eternal needs of people. Theodore O. Wedel points up this truth graphically,

> The Gospel is something more than a *bare* presentation of the person of Jesus. The Good News of salvation is a drama, an action—one in which the convert must participate. It must be preached in *action* as well as in words.[8]

It can be pointed out that most of the charitable deeds mentioned in the earlier part of this chapter have become commonplace, the performance of which is taken for granted in our polite society. The church cannot impress people, we are told, by caring for the sick or by ministering to the poor. Furthermore, the government and social agencies carry on most of this work that was formerly performed by Christian agencies. This means, some tell us, that the church has been robbed of both the opportunity and the glamor of charitable deeds.

This easygoing conclusion misses the point. It lacks insight into the present needs of individual men and of society. It is true that people in many parts of the world presently have fewer temporal and physical privations than they once had, but there is reason to believe that the human spirit is impoverished as much as ever. The high incidence of psychosomatic sickness indicates that the soul of man is ill, being attacked by fear, anxiety, frustration, a sense of futility, and boredom, all of which are as deadly as germs. The high number of nervous breakdowns resulting in mental illness testifies cogently to the needs of men's minds.

---

[8] Theodore O. Wedel, "Evangelism, An Essay in Criticism," *Ecumenical Review*, III (July, 1951), p. 367.

The church must discover creative ways of reaching the spiritually impoverished. The present wants, hopes, and needs of people are a concern to the church because they are a part of life and thus spiritually related. The task of ministering to the inner needs of man is difficult. It is easier to give a hungry man a loaf of bread or in modern practice, a relief check, than to minister to his impoverished spirit. Our generation is more successful in maintaining the physical health of our people than in keeping them mentally and spiritually well.

A broad interest in people's physical and temporal needs does not mean that the church is to be everybody's little chore boy. The church surely fritters away its strength and time by such a procedure. It should observe a twofold principle in this matter. First, it should have a genuine concern for people's present needs. Secondly, it must maintain a genuine spiritual motive in all of its work.

The church must express its concern for the physical and temporal needs of men in its worship, in social and civic action, and in a personal ministry of loving deeds.

First, the worship of the church must meet people's present needs. It is unrealistic to think that we can bypass the vexing problems of everyday life and minister effectively to men's eternal welfare. All of us are something like the down-and-out men who go to the downtown missions. It is hard to think of eternal things on an empty stomach—or with a mind filled with anxieties. While every part of corporate worship should have some relevance to men's present and eternal needs, perhaps the pastoral prayer and sermon offer the best opportunities for the expression of this concern.

The Reverend Jean K. Sherman of South Dakota prays for the schoolteachers in the fall and for the High School graduates in the spring. He also remembers the young people recently gone away to college. William Sangster, prominent Methodist minister in England, often prays for certain sick people by name, especially in his Sunday evening meeting. A Minnesota pastor prays for the road men who plow out the snowdrifts during the winter storms. A friend recently told me that a new compassion came to him as he heard his pastor pray for the doctor and nurses as they worked through the night in a nearby mental hospital. His concern also reached the patients in the hospital as the pastor prayed for "those troubled in mind and spirit." There are times when every person in every community especially needs prayer. Let the pastor be alert as to the times people especially stand in this need.

Moreover, preaching should be directed to help people with their present and eternal needs. This calls for life-situational preaching that has a genuine spiritual focus. Life-situational preaching is in bad repute in some groups inasmuch as they believe that it is antithetical to Biblical preaching. Nothing can be further from the truth. The Bible is the great textbook of life. Its materials come from actual life by the guardianship of the Holy Spirit. Its characters are not fictitious people stepping upon an imaginary stage and undertaking to dramatize life for us. They are real men and women, hard pressed at times, meeting actual problems of human existence. Jesus was a master in life-situational preaching and there can be no other effective type of pulpit ministry. If men's eternal needs are not dealt with in the context of their present urgent problems, it is likely that the minister's words have little relevance or effect.

Secondly, the church must have genuine concern and deep compassion for people who are suffering because of social injustice. If the church is quiet and passive in the presence of human need and tragedy it need not be surprised if it is rejected. Its sanctimonious words have little appeal to large numbers of people if it considers itself a neat little middle-class institution. It can claim no relationship to the Old Testament prophetic tradition if it is neutral or timid in protesting social evils that blight men's spirits and damn their souls. Many ministers are repudiating their prophetic heritage by a timorous spirit in the face of great social evils. A concern for social righteousness does not mean that a preacher must become a politician or a sociologist. He simply applies the Gospel of Christ to present conditions.

Thirdly, in addition to worship and social concern every preacher should maintain a virile person-to-person program of helpfulness. The church must continue many of the traditional forms of charity such as ministering to the poor, the care of the sick and counseling the frustrated. In doing this it does not become a competitor with the social agencies. It cares for those who have been overlooked, indeed, but it does its work differently, in a highly personal way that comes out of deep Christian concern. It expresses its love for the unfortunate, the poor, the sick and the sorrowing. It seeks out the anxious and frustrated and helps them by genuine spiritual fellowship.

There is evangelistic appeal in a comprehensive ministry when it is controlled by a genuine spiritual genius. Everyone can understand the rhetoric of loving deeds. On the other hand, many people misinterpret the direct evangelistic endeavors of churches believing that revival meetings and other evangelistic efforts are a type of ecclesiastical competition designed to gain supporters for local churches in order to increase their prestige in their communities.

In the fourth century of our era Christian benevolence had won so many adherents to the faith that when Julian the Apostate sought to re-establish the old pagan religions he deliberately copied the Christian plan of charity, hoping to win the populace back to the old Roman faiths. Julian, bitterly hating the Christians, unwittingly complimented them by imitation. On the other hand, his acrimonious words still testify to the evangelistic power of loving deeds. "Those Galileans," he complained, "feed not only their own poor, but ours; our poor lack our care." [9] In seeking to account for the phenomenal success of the Christian faith, he said, "This godlessness (*i.e.,* Christianity) is

[9] Adolf Harnack, *Mission and Expansion of Christianity*, Vol. 2 (New York: G. P. Putnam's Sons, 1902), p. 162.

mainly furthered by its philanthropy toward strangers and its careful attention to the bestowal of the dead." [10] Eusebius, first Christian historian, tells of the evangelistic appeal that came from the courageous and selfless work of the early Christians in a plague-ridden city.

> Then did they (the Christians) show themselves to the heathen in the clearest light. For the Christians were the only people who, amid such terrible ills, showed their fellow-feeling and humanity by their actions. Day by day some would busy themselves with attending to the dead and burying them (for there were numbers to whom no one else paid any heed); others gathered in the one spot all who were afflicted by hunger throughout the whole city and gave bread to them all. *When this became known, people glorified the Christians' God, and, convinced by the very facts, confessed that Christians alone were truly pious and religious.* (Ecclesiastical History 9:8.)

Evangelistic appeal and power inhere in a ministry of demonstrated love. God himself recognized this when he sent his Son into the world. Before Christ came, God had declared his love by his prophets but the people did not heed. In his infinite wisdom, he chose to demonstrate his concern for man by the Incarnation and the Cross. Jesus emphasized the evangelistic appeal of love when he said, "And I, when I am lifted up from the earth, will draw all men to myself" (John 12:32).

Every genuine Christian, though in a totally different sense, incarnates the love of God and expresses it in flesh and blood. In seeking to win men to Christ, Luther emphasized this viewpoint in saying, "and so will I give myself to be, as it were, a Christ to my neighbor, just as Christ has shown himself to me." (*Weimar Ausgabe,* Vii, 66, 3f.) The incarnation of Christ pleads for a continued ministry of demonstrated love.

---

[10] *Ibid.,* 165.

Making Ends Meet

9

The finances of many smaller congregations go from crisis to crisis with a series of urgent appeals for money to meet embarrassing deficits. The loyal laymen give generously out of a sense of honor in order to save the respect of the church or to keep the people in the parsonage from becoming hungry.

This type of desperation finance is destructive of morale. Every deficit suggests that the church is failing. Some of the donors become overly sensitive about their congregation's poverty and they conclude that sacrifice is unwarranted. They become suspicious of new projects, being fearful that they will be left holding the sack.

The basis for desperation financing is sometimes in an actual limited financial potential. In such cases the budget must be planned realistically in reference to the ability of the people to give. There are many churches, however, that carry on desperation financing that have a sufficiently large financial potential. In such cases there is usually a lack of stewardship education, short-time planning, and a poor presentation of the financial needs of the church to the congregation.

Educating for Stewardship

Thousands of churches in America, many of them smaller, carry on their financial programs on sub-Christian standards. They undertake to raise money with various selling plans and they ask for offerings and pledges on the basis of secular and worldly appeals. Such unspiritual practices account for many of the difficulties in church finance and for the impoverished spiritual condition of large numbers of professing Christians.

Plans of merchandising are ineffective usually as means of helping support the church. In the first place such plans frequently demand a disproportionate amount of time for the returns realized. Many ardent Christian women have found that the Ladies Aid did not receive twenty-five cents per hour for their strenuous efforts in preparing a church supper to raise money to pay the preacher. Again, some selling projects dishonor the church and her Lord. Rummage sales with their motley arrays of out-of-date hats, old clothes, and antedated furniture suggest that the Lord is in pretty bad shape financially. Finally, and most significantly, plans of merchandising to support the church discourage genuine stewardship. When such plans are used, the people are conditioned to believe that they can think up some ingenious plan of making the money instead of giving it. Church selling plans are spiritually sterile and psychologically bad.

There are churches that use other sub-Christian methods of raising money because they consider church finance as a business and not as a spiritual matter. Believing that the church must get money to carry on its program they overlook the spiritual opportunities in raising the money. Church officers make up the budget and they "assess" the members on their ability to pay much as tax commissioners do. In a few cases, the assessments are actually made and statements of what each member is expected to pay are sent out in the mails. In most cases, however, the "assessments" are less direct. The members of the church come to realize what is expected of them and they pledge accordingly out of a sense of obligation to the church and not out of a recognition of their stewardship to God.

Frequently congregations, many of them smaller, use high pressure sales methods to get the money to float a project or to pay a delinquent bill. These methods are often coercive and the use of them is always a short-sighted policy. Following such appeals laymen come to question the validity of their ecclesiastical investments. Moreover, coercive methods always miss the heart of stewardship. They result in people giving to an institution rather than giving out of a sense of gratitude to God.

Stewardship education provides the answers to churches that carry on their finances on sub-Christian standards. It emphasizes the spiritual values of thoughtful and sacrificial giving. It teaches that generous giving, especially tithing, is a means of grace as surely as corporate worship, Bible reading, and prayer. Stewardship education emphasizes that people need to give money for their own sakes as much as the church needs to receive it.

The matter of giving as a means of grace is deeply rooted. The Old Testament sacrifices had this element in them. Tithing itself arose in the Old Testament as an act of devotion and not as an expedient plan to support a temple or a priesthood. The element of devotion must be maintained in highly commercialized days when people are urged to give so that the church can carry on its business.

Sacrificial giving is to spiritual life what bodily exercise is to physical life. The Christian grows spiritually as he activates and actualizes the words and forms of his worship. Many moderns worship in a passive manner and they realize little from such services. Thousands of worshipers listen to prayers for the poor and they join in liturgies for the conversion of the heathen without feeling any genuine concern for either the poor or the heathen. Worshipers sometimes nod sanctimonious heads upon hearing the truth but often they do little about spreading abroad this truth. Generous giving is a type of active participation that develops spiritual life more greatly than hundreds of pious words spoken passively as the worshiper is borne along by the current of the service.

Stewardship education emphasizes that the love of money blocks spiritual growth. Most people remain small in personality because they do not give generously. Robert Merrick in one of Lloyd Douglas' stories was like that. His nurse once said of him, "You have something very valuable besides money but you will never use it. It is in you all right but it will never come out. Nobody will ever know that you had it. The money will be always blocking the way. '"[1]

Stewardship education emphasizes that the need for giving is deeply rooted in human nature. Man has an elemental need to share as surely as he has a need to associate with his fellows. God made him to be a responsible member of society with a capacity to be aware of his fellows' needs and with an impulse to help them. The refusal to help is a violation of his very nature and it develops egocentricity and a sense of frustration.

Stewardship education emphasizes that life is fulfilled by generous giving. A life of sharing relates one to his fellow men and it fosters growth of love. It gives life a deepened meaning for it extends one's influence beyond his little circle of affairs. The generous giver has a sense of self-esteem, though not pride, for he knows he is fulfilling God's purpose for him. The generous giver receives a rare quality of joy. The world's most genuine benefactors have usually been the world's most joyous people. Jesus emphasized this, as quoted by Paul, "It is more blessed to give than to receive" (Acts 20:35). Jesus was emphasizing that the giver gets more out of giving than does the one who receives.

Even the smallest congregation should employ a number of methods in their programs of stewardship education. Pastors should emphasize the stewardship of money in their preaching, knowing that Christ had a great deal to say about the right use of money. Pastors should give also a series of Bible Studies on stewardship in prayer meetings and in early Sunday evening group meetings. Sunday-school classes may often take a quarter to give attention to a systematic study of Christian stewardship using suitable textbooks and materials. Some churches

---

[1] Lloyd Douglas, *Magnificent Obsession* (Chicago: Willett, Clark and Company, 1929), p. 27.

have stewardship revivals that last for one week during which time there is a series of stewardship sermons and group discussions of man's accountability to God. There should be a stewardship secretary or committee that distributes stewardship literature, organizes stewardship reading clubs, and encourages stewardship reading by every effective means.

Instruction in stewardship should be followed by the practice of stewardship. This means that the people should be challenged to implement the principles they have learned. More specifically, the people should be challenged to tithe. Even after thorough instruction many people fear to commit themselves to a program of tithing. Where such a situation prevails the pastor can appeal for short-time commitments. There are some seasons of the year that are uniquely favorable for such an appeal. Perhaps the best time is the Lenten season. Advent weeks are also good. Sometimes short-time commitments for tithing can be obtained on the basis of present urgent needs in the church. Frequently people get so much joy out of tithing that they wish to continue.

Stewardship education not only lays a basis for spiritual growth in a church but it provides the most successful plan of financing a church from the standpoint of raising money. It does away with haphazard methods that are characterized by financial crises and emergencies. No church can be financed well that does not have a virile emphasis on stewardship. Gaines Dobbins says that trying to run a church on sporadic financial appeals is like trying to "raise a crop without regard to seed and soil and season." [2]

Raising the Budget

"The reason many people dislike to give is because they do it so poorly," says Willard Chitty, of Willard Chitty Associates. [3] This generalization, validated in the lives of thousands of

---

[2] Gaines Dobbins, The Church Book (Nashville: Broadman Press, 1951), p. 70.

[3] In a lecture in a class in Church Administration, Asbury Theological Seminary, April 27, 1956.

professing Christians, underscores the need of stewardship training, as we have already noted, and it points up the necessity of systematic giving to a well planned financial program. Haphazard giving is not personally rewarding. People want to give regularly to well planned budgets. Even the smallest church should have a budget that is raised by systematic giving.

The Sunday on which the annual budget is presented, often called Annual Stewardship Sunday or Loyalty Sunday, is judgment day for that church. In the first place, it is a judgment day on the quality of the stewardship education that has been carried on. Secondly, the people judge the effectiveness of the program of the past year. If their pledges for the new year are enthusiastic, and perhaps increased, they give a clear verdict that effective work has been done. A church that has carried on an effective program with children and youth, ministered helpfully in worship, provided meaningful fellowship and pastoral care, and reached out to the sinner, may anticipate raised pledges. On the other hand, if the giving is reluctant or diminished, other things being equal, the congregation gives a verdict of dissatisfaction about the achievements of the past. Thirdly, Loyalty Sunday is judgment day on the preparation and presentation of the annual budget. An enthusiastic response indicates, other things being equal, that the finance committee worked out a good budget, carried on effective publicity, and organized an appealing plan for the presentation of the financial needs of the church.

In anticipating Loyalty Sunday the finance committee should begin its work well in advance of that day. It has two basic tasks to perform. It must prepare the budget for the new year and it must present it to the people and obtain pledges.

The budget, as prepared by the finance committee and approved by the official board, must take into account the opportunities of service that confront the church as well as the financial potential of the congregation. This means that vision and business realism must work together in the formulation of the budget. If vision alone is regarded it is likely that an overly expanded program will be launched and the church will be involved in deficit spending and a disreputable financial record. Spiritual and financial integrity go together. A church cannot succeed spiritually and fail to keep its financial commitments. On the other hand, if the church, especially a smaller congregation, is run on a hardheaded business basis little can be accomplished. Vision and enthusiasm die and the church becomes as another business organization.

The pastor's salary is by far the most important item in the budget of the smaller church and it must be viewed realistically by the congregation. In former years people in some congregations assumed that the pastor, as a man of faith, might live on faith and the meager freewill offerings. They did not see that they should assure their minister of a salary and that the whole congregation should join in faith with their pastor for adequate support. This is the better way, for the faith of many is greater than the faith of one.

There are three other items that must have a high priority in the budget. First, there must be an item for the maintenance of the church property. Run down property nullifies the gospel of Christ. Secondly, there must be an allowance for local church extension and evangelism. If this is not done the church becomes only a vegetative social and religious institution. Thirdly, there must be an allowance for benevolence and missions beyond the local community. This is necessary for the church to save its own soul from egocentricity.

The finance committee presents the budget to the members and friends of the church and it obtains the pledges. The appeal for the pledges should be made on the basis of genuine stewardship. People are encouraged to relate their pledges to tithing. The appeal for the annual subscriptions may be made in one of three ways.

First, the budget may be presented in the morning worship service of the annual Loyalty Sunday or Stewardship Sunday.

This is the most usual way for smaller churches. With this plan a layman explains the budget, often after the pastor's sermon on stewardship, and an appeal is made for pledges. Pledge cards have usually been distributed and these are signed and brought to the altar where the pastor prays for God's blessing on the church and on the people as they support it. This plan assumes that adequate preparation and publicity have assured a large congregation. After the finest publicity, however, some of the prospective contributors will not have been present and a team of personal workers will need to call on the absentees. This should be done immediately so that the budget can be pledged by the following Sunday.

Secondly, other congregations have their annual Loyalty day services but they receive no pledges at that time. On that Sunday afternoon teams of personal workers go to assigned members and friends and secure their pledges. The persons who could not be seen in the first canvass are visited the following week so that the budget can be subscribed completely by the following Sunday. This plan assumes also good publicity as well as a corps of carefully selected and well organized callers.

Thirdly, small churches can sometimes most profitably promote and present their budgets through their Sunday-school classes. For two or three weeks prior to Loyalty Sunday the matter of the church budget is discussed. Literature is sent home to the parents who are not members of the Sunday school or attendants at the worship services. Each class accepts a goal to raise under the direction of the teacher and a spirit of friendly competition is encouraged. On Loyalty Sunday all of the pledges are brought to the classes and a report is made of the results. The achievements of the Sunday-school classes are reported in the Loyalty Sunday church service and the budget is presented there so that those who were not in Sunday school have an opportunity to pledge. The whole worship service, quite naturally, centers around Christian stewardship. Teams of lay visitors call on the constituents who were absent from both Sunday school and morning worship and their pledges are received.

This plan assumes a unified budget that includes Sunday school and church monies. Offerings for the unified budget are taken in Sunday school and all attendants, including adults, make their contributions. A report of the offerings of the classes and of the Sunday school as a whole may be made. An offering is taken in the worship service, quite naturally, for those who were not in the church school.

This plan has some distinct advantages for smaller congregations because they often have Sunday schools that are larger than their church memberships. I know a church with fifty adult members that has a Sunday school of more than two hundred in average attendance. The influence of that little church is great in its community and many of the parents of the Sunday-school children wish to support the work. Their contributions can be received most easily by offerings that are brought by the children to the Sunday-school classes.

Providing Adequate Plant and Facilities

The smaller church faces a difficult problem in the matter of providing an adequate plant and adequate facilities. Thousands of smaller congregations need to plan immediately for advance along these lines. Some of them have shown little growth because they have been getting along with inadequate space. Others are having a good growth, especially in their Sunday schools and youth work, but they must now build additions if they are to continue to grow. Expansion of plant is usually difficult for the little congregations because growth is frequently most pronounced in the Sunday school and little financial help can be expected from that department.

Every congregation that considers an expansion or a renovation of its plant should ask three pertinent questions. Affirmative answers to these questions validate the project. First, is there essential agreement in the congregation as to what should be done by way of building or improvement? Secondly, is the proposed project within the financial ability of the church? Finally, is there essential agreement in the congregation regarding the money-raising campaign that must be carried on?

Local churches, even smaller ones, are increasingly turning to professional money raising organizations to raise funds for expansion and improvement projects. There are many such organizations and one can be employed to raise funds for various small projects. Some of the organizations have contracts that provide as little as three days of professional service in the matter of heading up a money raising campaign in small churches. The minimum fee for such service is about $300.00. Most of the fund raising organizations, quite naturally, prefer projects calling for large sums of money with larger fees.

There are normally four phases in fund raising campaigns. There is a period of *preparation* which includes clarification of objectives, the start of the publicity, and the selection of committees. The second phase is the *selection and organization* of the lay solicitors. These people are indoctrinated in the validity and necessity of the building or improvement project. The solicitors make their own pledges as objective evidence that they support heartily the campaign. Thirdly, the solicitors are *trained* in the principles of successful solicitation of funds. Finally, the solicitors go out two by two and *canvass* the church families for their gifts.

Many smaller churches do not find it wise to employ the services of professional fund raising organizations. This policy is especially wise if the majority of the members are loyal and active. Professional services in raising money are often most helpful in big congregations that have large numbers of semi-interested and inactive members.

Some smaller congregations make an effective substitute for professional services in this matter by engaging a successful fund raising minister, perhaps of their own denomination, to assist them. Such a man is frequently a pastor who obtains a short leave from his church for such an activity. At other times he is related to the denominational evangelistic or church extension board and spends full time in raising money for local churches under the direction of the general board. In other cases, pastors make a thorough study of the principles of raising building funds and they direct their own campaigns.

There are churches that prefer to start raising money well in advance of an anticipated building project by methods other than the direct subscriptions of their people. These methods are numerous and they are sometimes promoted by the church as a whole and at other times by one or more of the departments. Special attention should be given here to two closely related methods that have been helpful to many smaller congregations.

The Lord's Acre Plan has been outstandingly successful in rural areas in raising money for expansion projects. In this plan farmers dedicate to the Lord a crop upon a specified plot of ground. Sometimes growing animals are given also to God in the Lord's Acre plan. In the fall, after harvest, all the proceeds from the Lord's Acre projects are brought to the church in a great Harvest festival. The Lord's Acre plan seldom reduces the amount of money pledged regularly to the church budget. It is not only an effective means of raising money for special projects but it tends to make sacred the growing of crops and animals for those who participate in it.

The God's Portion plan is a companion method to the Lord's Acre that can be used in villages and cities. Here the members dedicate a specific portion of their income to God in addition to their budget giving. A factory worker, for instance, gives the wages for the first two hours work of each week. A salaried worker gives his salary for the first day or two of the month to be used in a special project. Merchants sometimes give the profits from sales for a specified period to assist in a building campaign. Dedicated Christians follow God's Portion plan, or the Lord's Acre, in addition to tithing. This represents a high sense of stewardship.

OVER
TITHE

It often happens that smaller churches are overly cautious about inaugurating plans for expansion. Thousands of congregations have missed forever opportunities for service and growth because of overly conservative attitudes along this line. In such cases it has been argued, and successfully, that the congregation was not meeting its budget and that a campaign for building funds was unrealistic. Many times, however, the church had a financial potential that had not been challenged because of a lack of vision and faith. Most official boards do not know that budget offerings often increase when a needed and realistic building campaign is launched. The reason for this phenomenon is valid. People like to give to an enterprising and a growing institution.

Positive attitudes are basic to successful church finance. The pastor and his financial officers must have a constructive outlook in this matter. They must not be apologetic about urging the people to practice the principles of Christian stewardship. They must see clearly that in these days of secularism wholehearted tithing is a means *par excellence* for personal growth in grace. Moreover, for successful church finance there must be confidence in the people's willingness to give. Negative attitudes along this line are self-defeating. Furthermore, there must be a success-mindedness about the mission and the program of the church. Many churches are defeated because they have the attitude of a defeatest. Smaller churches should not quench a spirit of adventure and faith that calls for reasonable Christian sacrifice. The Kingdom of God is not built by those who are looking for easy paths and indulgent living.

Personalizing Publicity   10

"It is difficult for our church to make much progress," said a frustrated lay leader in a little church located in a small city. "For one thing," he continued, "we can't advertise because of the lack of funds." The layman made a twofold observation about church publicity. In the first place, as a successful business man, he observed correctly that advertising is important in today's church work. In the second place he observed incorrectly that all publicity is expensive.

Every local church can have effective publicity irrespective of the size of its advertising budget. As a matter of fact, the best type of advertising, especially for smaller churches, costs little in dollars and cents. It is achieved in large part by having a well organized plan of publicity based on congregational enthusiasm for the work of the church.

The smaller church must specialize in personalized publicity. This should be the genius and basis of its advertising. Personalized publicity, quite obviously, represents a type that is highly friendly and informal, and it stands in contrast to impersonal and formal publicity as found in newspaper ads, radio announcements and church signs. There are two types of personalized publicity that are uniquely important to smaller churches: person-to-person or word-of-mouth publicity of the members and friends of the church; and regular personalized mail sent to the constituency.

The smaller church must carry on also some types of advertising that are not highly personal. It needs to give attention to newspaper stories and ads, especially in smaller communities, and it should use a few selected types of permanent advertisements.

Before discussing the various types of advertising we should observe that all publicity must rest upon a worthy church program. Occasionally a preacher, sometimes a younger man, gets bitten by the publicity bug. Perhaps he has taken a course or read a book on church advertising and he believes that the hope of the Kingdom lies in effective publicity. He announces sermon topics that promise more than is delivered. He glamorously advertises services that turn out to be dull. He writes glowing news stories of little achievements. After a few months he finds that his work is failing and he becomes a disillusioned preacher. The failure, of course, was with the poor program that nullified every effort along other lines.

Person-to-Person Publicity

The genuine interest and enthusiasm that the members have for their church are basic factors in the person-to-person type of publicity. "When the members of the church express spontaneously great happiness in the fellowship of the church, that church will have congregations whether it employs unique methods of advertising or not." [1] On the other hand, there is little effective word-of-mouth publicity if the people do not recognize genuine merit in the church's worship and in its program generally. No amount of pastoral exhortation causes the people to publicize their church if the worship services are poorly ordered, the singing uninspired and flat, and the preaching dull. As noted above, the results are nil if the members do invite outside people to such services. Cashman correctly observes, "even free publicity is practically useless unless there is a worthy church program with definite goals to be reached." [2]

[1] J. A. Biebe, *The Pastoral Office* (New York: Methodist Book Concern, 1923), p. 228.
[2] Robert Cashman, *The Business Administration of the Church* (New York: Willett, Clark and Co., 1937), p. 46.

The people of most congregations, however, do not properly publicize their churches unless some creative plan is used to inspire person-to-person announcements. Many churches have found it necessary to organize for word-of-mouth publicity. The De Witt Memorial Church in New York City, along with other congregations, has block captains who visit the unchurched people of their blocks periodically and invite them to church. A few years ago, Joseph Sizoo doubled his congregation at the New York Avenue Church in Washington within one year by having an organized group of his men invite several people each week to the services. Warner P. Davis greatly increased his Sunday evening congregations at the Epworth Methodist Church in Lexington, Kentucky, by using the Pew Plan. With this simple plan, church families accepted the responsibility of bringing enough people to fill one or more pews assigned to them for the given services. Many pastors have clubs of selected persons whose task is to call regularly upon the unchurched and invite them to the meetings. An evening during the week is spent regularly for this work.

Some pastors use telephone brigades to good advantage. A few years ago a pastor in Denver had a brigade so well organized that he could contact his constituency of more than six hundred or seven hundred people within a period of two hours. To do this he called his ten captains, each of whom called five or six lieutenants. Each of the five or six lieutenants called five or six families or persons. This plan made it possible to reach three hundred or more families with a minimum of work for everybody. Many of the little churches can operate well with three or four captains, instead of ten.

In commenting on telephone brigades or squadrons, Rockwell Smith suggests that they be composed of older women who are no longer able to be active in many other church affairs. Smith points out that usually these women have a deep loyalty to the church and that they are eager to serve. He moreover suggests, with a kindly touch of sarcasm, that "they know the gossip channels of the community and are in a position to use them creatively." [3] In using a telephone squadron, the pastor provides the text of an announcement to each of the captains who relay it in an informal and friendly manner.

Person-to-person publicity is the method *par excellence* in the Christian Church. It strengthens the public announcements and invitations by the interest and concern of Christian personality. It was used almost solely by the church for many centuries before the advent of modern advertising. George E. Sweazey reports that it is working with outstanding effectiveness in Spain. Protestant churches in that country are not permitted to advertise, not even by a bulletin board reading, "Preaching at 11:00 a.m." No cross nor Christian symbol may be used to mark the Protestant meeting places. The evangelical churches rely wholly on person-to-person advertising. Yet, under such restrictions, Protestantism is prospering in Spain with its membership having doubled or tripled in the last few years. [4]

Using the Mailing List

The mail carrier in every community is waiting to help pastors build up their congregations by delivering personalized mail. In smaller churches such mail consists of pastoral letters and cards, announcements and promotional letters, and perhaps a weekly or monthly news sheet.

Every pastor should build and maintain an ever enlarging mailing list. He needs this as much as he needs his automobile. The list should include the names of church members, all the families that are represented in the Sunday school and every other church department, irregular church attendants, and every unchurched person in the immediate community. The names should be obtained from the rolls of all the church departments, the community canvass, visitors at the church, and from lists of

[3] Rockwell Smith, *Rural Church Administration* (Nashville: Abingdon-Cokesbury, 1953), p. 78.

[4] Cf. W. A. Pleuthner, *More Power for Your Church* (New York: Farrar, Strauss, and Young, 1952), p. 4.

prospects provided by the church members. G. B. Williamson suggests that such a list should be divided into three classifications:

> a large list of persons to whom occasional announcements may be sent; a more select list to whom all publicity of general interest may be forwarded; and an exclusive list of friends, prospects and members who, because of hindering circumstances, are unable to be in regular attendance, to whom the church bulletins and all printed announcements may be mailed weekly.[5]

Many pastors give special attention to the writing of personal letters to their members and church attendants. The pastor of a Mennonite church in Los Angeles spends time every Monday morning going over his mailing list and writing notes to his people. Sometimes his notes express appreciation for fine services rendered the day before. At other times they express regret that the person had not been able to attend the meetings. Sometimes the letters carry a short account of some special achievement in the services. Frequently these missives announce some special feature in the services on the following Sunday. Another pastor gives special attention to writing letters of congratulation, taking note of special anniversary days and the times when honors have come. Still another pastor makes it a special point to write to the members who are temporarily absent from the church, especially young people at college.

Personal pastoral notes and letters have much value when they are thoughtfully written. They are a graphic demonstration of the thoughtfulness and concern of the pastor. Andrew Blackwood believes that ministers often underestimate the value people put on letters simply because they themselves receive so much mail. To the humble people, particularly, "the coming of

---

[5] G. B. Williamson, *Overseers of the Flock* (Kansas City: Beacon Hill, 1952), p. 205.

a brief note, written in ink and signed by the most beloved man in town may constitute an event." [6]

Because of time limitations, many pastors use a more formal and stereotyped kind of letter. These letters normally bear announcements to the church constituency or they promote some special project. They are sent only when there is definite and significant need for them. Some of the people start throwing the envelopes unopened into the waste paper basket if the pastor writes uninteresting letters on trivial matters.

Even form letters may have personalized elements. The letter itself should be written in a friendly and informal manner. If multigraphed, the sender's name and address, along with a personal salutation may be typed at the head of the letter. Increased personal value is given the letter if it is signed by the pastor and sent by first class mail.

There is a fine art in writing effective promotional letters and every pastor ought to give this matter thought until he excels in it. Stewart Harral holds that every effective letter has at least "five basic objectives. It should (1) get attention, (2) arouse interest, (3) create desire, (4) establish conviction, and (5) get action." [7]

Many smaller churches are getting good results from mid-week reminders. These four-page folders, often like a church bulletin in appearance, are sent out in the middle of the week with the purpose of announcing and promoting the program of the church, especially on the following Sunday. Churches with a mailing list of a hundred family names should consider using such a publication, especially if secretarial help is available in the church. The value becomes somewhat more dubious if the pastor himself must do the mimeographing and mailing. In any event, the mimeographing must be of high quality.

---

[6] Andrew Blackwood, *Pastoral Work* (Philadelphia: Westminster, 1945), p. 140.

[7] Stewart Harral, *Successful Letters for Churches* (Nashville: Abingdon-Cokesbury, 1946), p. 16.

Some pastors use their church bulletins as publicity sheets by having them printed or mimeographed by the middle of the week and then sent to at least a part of their mailing list. Such a practice unites the functions of the midweek reminder and the church bulletin. The bulletin carries the order of the worship services for the following Sunday, makes announcements of all meetings, carries news notes, and presents other pertinent material. Page four of the bulletin can be used for informational and promotional material such as the history, beliefs and standards of the church; a short personal message by the pastor; or the presentation of a project or the report of an achievement. The enlarged use of the church bulletin is of significant interest and value to smaller congregations.

A few smaller congregations publish a parish paper that is issued monthly or bi-monthly. Such a paper is larger than the midweek reminder and more space is devoted to the program of the church, news notes and devotional material. The expediency of publishing a monthly parish paper depends upon a number of factors including the finances of the church, the size of the mailing list and the availability of qualified secretarial help.

Could it be handed out until finances are available

Getting in the Newspapers

Most of the newspaper editors actually want church news—contrary to the opinions of many pastors. The situation could not be otherwise because editors need news. It is their stock in trade. Moreover they need church news inasmuch as churches are important institutions in every community. In these days of religious awakening an increasingly large number of people are interested in the religious life of their areas.

It is important, however, that churches recognize clearly the meaning of *news*. Several decades ago Willard G. Bleyer, for many years director of the School of Journalism at the University of Wisconsin, gave a definition that has become classic. "News is anything that is timely that interests a number of people; and the best news is that which has the greatest interest for the greatest number." [8] Most editors look at news articles from that perspective.

Many smaller churches might have more news stories in their papers if they would give the matter careful attention. This is true especially in communities with weekly, semi-weekly, and small daily papers. Even in sizable communities it may be assumed that smaller churches might have as many as twenty-five or thirty news stories every year in addition to their regular church announcements. A brief survey of the possibilities validates this viewpoint.

In the first place, stories of elections make good articles. Not only should a story of the annual church election be reported but articles of the election of Sunday-school officers and teachers, and the officers of other departments should be sent to the newspaper. Secondly, every smaller church has a number of good stories every year about special speakers and services. These stories should announce the special service normally rather than carry an account of the event. Thirdly, stories of special projects should be given publicity. These may include building and improvement projects, support of a missionary or missionary interests, or some other newsworthy activity. Fourthly, sermons that confront community problems may be reported. If the pastor said something in his sermon in which many people are interested, it is likely that the editor will print a story on the sermon. Holt McPherson points out that "the utterances of a pastor on Sunday are just as important to many readers as the talk of a visiting speaker at the civic club or the remarks of the farm agent at the 4-H Club banquet." [9] Fifthly, newspapers often carry stories of denominational meetings and achievements when they are reported by local churches that participated in the events. Finally, achievements should be re-

---

[8] Willard G. Bleyer, *Newspaper Writing and Editing* (Boston: Houghton Mifflin, 1913), p. 18.

[9] Holt McPherson, *Churchmen, Let's Go to Press* (Nashville: Commission on Public Relations and Methodist Information, n.d.), p. 5.

ported. Highly newsworthy stories can be submitted by smaller churches on their giving to missions with a note of their per capita giving. Many smaller churches can submit superbly fine articles on their Sunday schools and other departments that are doing impressive work.

In most cases the pastor of a smaller church finds it necessary that he, personally, report the news. He must thus develop a news-mindedness much as he has a sermon-mindedness. Attention to this important matter pays high dividends for the time it takes. There are churches, however, that have laymen who are news-minded and are qualified to act as church reporters. In such cases these persons should be appointed to that important work.

Some churches have many of their news stories rejected because they are poorly written. In many cases the rejected articles have significant news items but the busy editor does not have time to rewrite the story. Attention to a few simple rules can remedy greatly this matter.

1. The pastor should identify the origin of the story by putting something like the following in a top corner of the first page: From John L. Smith, Pastor

The Community Church
462 North Washington Street
Telephone: 1234
For immediate release February 1, 1957

2. It is not necessary to start the story with a headline inasmuch as the editor has to write headlines to fit into the type of space he selects.

3. The leading paragraph should start about one-third of the way down the page and it should contain all of the essentials of the story. The best way to do this is to tell the who, what, when, where, and why in the fewest words. The following is an example of a lead paragraph:

The Rev. John White, evangelist of Chicago, Illinois, will speak at the opening service of a revival meeting tomorrow evening, at 7:30 p.m. in the Community Church.

4. The lead paragraph should be followed by other paragraphs that state details about the meeting. The pastor is named and, perhaps, his work in the meeting is indicated or he is quoted concerning some of the plans. The evangelist is further introduced. Special emphases and services are set forth.

5. It is highly advantageous to get news stories to the editor well in advance of the deadline. This gives added assurance that they will be included inasmuch as the busy editor can give careful attention to them.

Many weekly newspapers accept feature articles from pastors about their churches and about religion in general. Newspapers frequently carry articles on the history of local churches, particularly at the time of their anniversaries. Some pastors have written series of short, interesting articles about their denominations and local churches. Others have written short and pithy articles about religious living in general. Still others have had articles carried on some of the great Christian beliefs that are affirmed by their own churches along with others.

There are smaller local churches that find it profitable to carry regular paid ads in the newspapers. In most cases, however, the cost is too great to warrant this expenditure. It frequently happens that a little church can advertise its services more effectively by direct mail than by paid ads. Blackwood believes that newspaper ads do more to increase attendance at special services, or at series of meetings, than at the regular times of worship. His "rule" is especially relevant to smaller churches.

In a residential district the following rule may hold: Always advertise a special service, and never any other. For much the same reason a grocer calls attention to something new on his shelves, not to the staples such as flour and sugar. He does not advertise the main part of his stock in trade, but promotes items such as seasonable fruits.[10]

There are smaller churches, of course, that should carry paid ads regularly in the newspapers. Observance of a few simple criteria increases the effectiveness of such ads. In the first place, the ads should not be crowded. White space is valuable in display advertisements. Secondly, it increases effectiveness to use regularly a slogan or a symbol. A vivid slogan or the drawing of a cross or a church spire does much to get attention. Finally, sermon topics, if announced, should be vivid and appealing. They must be true, but, like headlines, they must have the ability to get people's attention.

Using Permanent Advertisements

Most smaller churches should use some types of permanent advertisements. Street and highway markers are often valuable. Listing in telephone and newspaper directories assists interested people to locate churches. Calendars and blotters remind people often of a church and its program. The results of these types of permanent publicity seem small but in the long run the gains are sometimes significant.

Bulletin boards offer possibilities for publicity as well as for an effective community ministry otherwise. Stanley I. Stuber maintains that one of the most valuable functions of the bulletin board is seen in its preaching ability. It can preach daily to hundreds that pass the church on their way to school, the shops, and the stores by presenting a short and effective message. This message should be presented in the first part of the week, beginning with Monday morning. In the middle of the week the church announcements for the following Sunday may be put up.

---

[10] Andrew Blackwood, *Pastoral Leadership* (Nashville: Abingdon-Cokesbury, 1949), p. 130.

The location of bulletin boards is important. They are normally, and quite properly, found on the church grounds in front of the church. It is sometimes advantageous to supplement the bulletin board located on the church site by one that is situated in a strategic place in the downtown area. In Bloomington, Wisconsin, the Methodist church, located in a residential area, maintains a bulletin board down on the main street of the village on a lot adjoining the Post Office. Several years ago a Christian business man, L. L. Bingham, of Estherville, Iowa, maintained six well-located bulletin boards in the business section of that county seat town. These boards proclaimed vital messages of Christian truth to about 10,000 people every week.

Church publicity is a holy art and an important ministry. It has a close relationship to the Biblical injunction, "Publish the glad tidings." The minister who advertises his church truthfully need not fear that he is playing the role of a publicity seeker. The church that is to meet its responsibilities today must interpret itself, its problems, its objectives and ideals. A church's publicity program must be the product of careful planning on the part of the pastor and his official board. Hit-and-miss publicity accomplishes little.

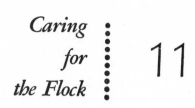

*Caring
for
the Flock*

11

Every pastor must be a specialist in human relations if he is to succeed. For maximum effectiveness he must be able to anticipate needs, interpret wishes, diagnose motives, and above all else, work harmoniously with people. This is especially true of smaller churches because, as noted above, personal relationships are generally more intimate and basic there than in large congregations. The people of smaller churches expect their pastors to be genuinely friendly and have a vital interest in all of the people as persons. The pastor of a large congregation may succeed as a distinguished pulpiteer or as a capable administrator, but a failure to carry on effective pastoral relations in a small church nullifies every other effort.

There is usually a basic difference in the pastoral work in large and smaller churches. The pastors in large churches are concerned primarily with "crisis situations," as Wayne Oates calls them.[1] Pastors of large congregations visit the sick, the dying, the bereaved and frustrated, but unless their churches are unusually well staffed they have little time for calling on people who do not have specific and apparent needs. Pastors of smaller churches, on the other hand, supplement their ministry in crisis situations with a plan of regular visitation of their people.

A part of the strength of the smaller church is in its regu-

---

[1] Wayne Oates, *The Christian Pastor* (Philadelphia: Westminster, 1951) pp. 13-23.

lar pastoral work. The results of regular or routine pastoral visitation are great. It establishes rapport between the pastor and the people. It personalizes the pastor's messages and his work of administration. It leads to a discovery of personal needs and it provides counseling opportunities for their solution. A genuinely effective church program cannot be carried on by public worship and group work alone. There are many individual spiritual needs that cannot be met in a corporate situation just as most individual physical needs cannot be met by a physician getting a group together and handing each of them a pill. "One patient at a time," has become a well established practice in medicine. The principle is relevant also in the care of souls.

Defining the Pastoral Personality

An understanding of human nature is basic to effective pastoral work. Ineffective pastors frequently do not understand human nature in general or individual persons in particular. Bishop L. R. Marston, of the Free Methodist Church, has shown, on the basis of a careful survey, that "problem pastors" often fail in the matter of "getting along with others and leading them without friction." [2] These men often know their theology better than they know their psychology and, sometimes, they are better acquainted with God than with their fellows. Effective pastors, on the other hand, know both God and man. Their knowledge of human nature and their understanding of persons are usually expressed in four basic traits that define an effective pastoral personality.

First, effective pastors are person-minded. Several years ago Richard Henry Edwards wrote a book entitled, *A Person-Minded Ministry,* in which he declared person-mindedness to be a fundamental attitude for ministerial success. In suggesting this, Edwards surely laid hold of the genius of a pastor's

or EVANGELISTS

---

[2] Leslie R. Marston, "Why Do Pastors Succeed? or Fail?" *The Christian Minister,* I (Spring, 1949), pp. 8-11.

work. Person-mindedness, defined as interest in persons as individuals, is the organizing center of a pastor's work. It is at the very heart of his person-to-person service. It is important also in preaching for the pastor preaches to persons. It is fundamental in church administration for he works with people there.

Person-mindedness does not come to be in a minister by some automatic process. As a matter of fact, many ministers, even pastors, do not have a keen interest in people as individuals. Some of the clergy have selected second best ministerial motives and less valuable integrative principles. There are preachers, particularly the pulpiteers, who are *idea-minded;* others, most especially the church administrators, are *promotion-minded* or *organization-minded.* The scholarly teacher type is likely to be *knowledge-minded.* Many liturgically trained ministers become *form-minded.* Every minister at times is tempted to be *ambition-minded.* When the going is hard, preachers may become *problem-minded.* None of these, however good some of them may be, are sufficiently valuable to take the place of *person-mindedness* in a shepherd of souls.

Person-mindedness provides the drive for an effective person-to-person ministry. It makes the pastor's association with his people a delight to him and to them. It makes his regular pastoral calling a challenging matter because people are as interesting to him as the latest book. It helps him to discover interests in the dullest and most prosaic of persons. With an attitude of person-mindedness pastors often see living dramas more exciting than any television can show. It makes the preacher's preaching relevant to living people, hard pressed by the rugged facts of life. The pastor of a large church, perhaps compensating by pulpit ability or administrative genius, can get by more easily without an attitude of person-mindedness than the pastor of a small church. This attitude is indispensable in groups where close interpersonal relationships are found.

Secondly, the ability to empathize is essential for an effective person-to-person ministry. This ability, like person-mindedness itself, is deeply rooted in the pastor's personality. It arises out of a deep concern for persons that is akin to compassion. Empathy, to use an old expression, is the ability to put one's self in the other fellow's shoes. It is the projection of one's self into another's situation or the acceptance of his perspective. Empathy does not have as much emotional content as sympathy. The former suggests "the ability to appreciate the other person's feelings without you yourself becoming so emotionally involved that your judgment is affected." [8]

Empathy is basic to rapport which, in person-to-person work, is the favorable spiritual-psychological climate of the interview. Empathy assures people that one cares enough to look at their problem as they see it. Empathy tells people of one's acceptance of them and helps to drive away a sense of personal isolation. Many persons in modern life are like a student on a large university campus who said, "I feel like a 'D minus' walking around on two legs."

Empathy is foundational to good listening. This is important because there can be little creative pastoral work unless the pastor is a good listener. The primary need of persons who are frustrated by unfounded fears, guilt feelings, irrational anxieties, and morbid dread is to have an opportunity to recount fully to a sympathetic pastor. They receive insight into their situation as they analyze their problems and acknowledge their feelings and attitudes. This procedure often results in an immediate solution of the difficulty. A contemporary college teacher and counselor recently gave an example of this phenomenon. A college boy had come to her for counsel. The student started to relate his difficulty, but after saying a few words he became very emotional and began to speak in a low voice and in an inarticulate manner. The counselor asked the

[8] John Kord Lagemann, "How's Your Empathy?" *The Christian Century* (February 23, 1959), p. 238.

young man to repeat what he had said. He started again but after a few sentences he spoke in a low voice again. The counselor then explained that her hearing was poor and she requested the young man to speak clearly and loudly. The student started his story again but only repeated the manner of the other times. The counselor did not ask the youth to repeat again but sat attentively while feigning comprehension. Upon finishing the story the young man became composed, arose, and thanked the counselor for solving his problem for him. On referring to this incident several months later, the counselor remarked that she had not learned at the time, nor later, what the young man's problem was. The counselor's helpfulness in providing the student a favorable opportunity to outline his problem brought personal insight.

Thirdly, the quality *par excellence* for the Christian minister is love of people. Love does more to qualify a man for effective Christian service than anything else (I Corinthians 13). In pastoral work, as in romance or family life, love covers a multitude of limitations and even, perhaps, some ministerial blundering. A pastor is on his own indeed if he will not genuinely love his people. They will find it hard to be tolerant and generous with his pastoral miscues.

Upon being appointed to a new congregation several years ago, I asked the presiding bishop of the conference, William Pearce, what he would do if he were then accepting a pastorate. I had assumed the bishop might outline a program that would indicate some basic principles that he considered of primary importance. The wise bishop said succinctly, "I would love my people." Out of his long perspective Bishop Pearce had come to believe that pastoral love was at the very heart of any successful pastoral work.

Christian love has two essential elements. These are indicated by two Greek words that are translated *love* in the New Testament. The first one, *agape,* indicates respect, esteem, and appreciation for the work of another. The word primarily indicates the rational aspects of love. The other term in the New Testament is *phileo* and it indicates the sentiments of love. It is primarily emotional in tone and refers to the feelings of love. As in marriage, both of these elements are necessary for the pastor. He must have the highest respect and esteem for his people and he must actually love them from his heart.

Many social psychologists have told us that people want nothing more than love and appreciation. Genuine pastoral love gives a creative tone to everything that the pastor does in the church. No pastor needs to announce from his pulpit that he appreciates and loves his people. Even adults, like babies, can sense when they are loved.

Finally, a rare brand of patience is needed for pastors in smaller churches. This is true especially when progress is slow. In speaking of Richard Baxter, Charles Kemp says,

> Some of the attitudes which carried into his work would bear direct evaluation, for example, his emphasis on patience. Of all the qualities necessary for pastoral care none is more essential than patience. It has been said that as many men fail in pastoral work from lack of patience as from any other thing.[4]

Genuine patience is not rooted in nonchalance, but rather it arises from confidence, hope and optimism. It is an expectant patience that banishes discouragement. Such a constructive attitude must be had in reference to persons as well as to slow-responding churches. Olin Curtis emphasizes the importance of such an attitude in reference to people.

> You hold a certain noble ideal over against a certain man—that he shall be a Christian of the largest and profoundest kind—and steadily you bear toward this man without dropping the ideal, and without weakening the demand. To yourself you say, day after day,

---

[4] Charles F. Kemp, *Physicians of the Soul* (New York: Macmillan, 1947), pp. 91, 92. Used by permission.

and perhaps year after year: "Ah, you cannot deceive me. I will believe in you more deeply than your own estimate. And I will not be satisfied with any makeshift. You simply must be *this other man* which I have in mind." The important thing is not how this bearing is expressed; the important thing is that *you really have it,* that you cultivate it, that you never give it up either before men or before God.[5]

The lack of pastoral patience and endurance has hindered some churches for a generation. They have become deeply scarred because a pastor lost his heart and abandoned a church in discouragement. Other men have become discouraged and stayed at their charges but inwardly they rejected the people. I once knew a young man, eager for immediate success in his church, who planned a revival meeting in the early months of his pastorate in a good but slow-moving church. The meeting was widely advertised and careful preparation was made for it. The meeting was held but there was little response and no converts. Deeply discouraged, the young pastor went to his pulpit with an air of prophetic authority and announced, "Little can be accomplished in this church. It has no future." It is a wonder that the official board did not demand that young man's resignation. His loss of hope after six months of inexperienced pastoral work might have justified such action.

Hear the parable of three hens. Each of them, ranging in a farm lot, decided that she would steal out her nest in a nearby thicket. The first hen, impatient and impulsive, after having laid the eggs, thought within herself, "If there is any good within these eggs, I am going to have it now." So she broke the eggs and ate them. The second decided that she would lay a nest of eggs, sit upon them, and finally have a brood of chickens. But she was an awkward old hen and stumbled over her eggs, breaking some of them and spoiling the others. The

---

[5] Olin A. Curtis, *The Christian Faith* (New York: The Methodist Book Concern, 1905) pp. 347-348.

third hen, patient and wise, decided that she also wished a brood of chickens. She was faithful in her sitting and skillful in getting on and off from the nest. After twenty-one days she was pleased as new life came from the shells.

It is like that with pastoral work. Sometimes we have broken situations by being impatient and impulsive and by demanding that we realize immediately any good in a pastoral situation. At other times, perhaps by being awkward and blundering, we have broken lives that we had hoped to save. But perhaps all of us can see, thank God, certain times when we have been patient, wise and skillful in difficult pastoral situations. In due time new spiritual life, both individual and corporate, has come forth because of the constancy of love and patience.

Organizing Pastoral Work

A wide variety of ministerial tasks, especially in smaller churches, tends to make pastors like Stephen Leacock's famous rider who, "flung himself upon his horse and rode madly off in all directions." Such a plight is occasioned usually by a lack of organization that results in crowding out important tasks, most especially pastoral calling.

Sometimes pastors, when in a confidential mood, confess to their fellows that they have a persistent sense of guilt because they do not call on their people as they believe that they should. A bishop stated recently that the pastor's sense of guilt is justified. He said that, in his experience, laymen complain more about their pastors' failure to call regularly than about anything else. Russell Dicks underscores this observation, "It is safe to say that eighty-five per cent or ninety per cent of the clergymen today are doing little effective pastoral work or personal counseling of any kind." [*]

It is true, indeed, that most preachers place a high priority

---

[*] Russell L. Dicks, *Pastoral Work and Personal Counseling* (New York: MacMillan, 1944), p. 4.

on their pastoral ministry to people in crisis situations. They call on the sick, the dying, the bereaved, and on others who are in trouble as soon as they learn of their needs. Effective pastors maintain a bearing and attitudes that suggest that they are eager always to help their people at any hour of day or night. They, moreover, encourage their people to contact them immediately when a crisis arises.

Pastors generally recognize that crisis situations constitute their primary responsibilities and, at the same time, their greatest opportunities. There are surely few things that are more inexcusable for a pastor than to be preoccupied or unconcerned so that he neglects those in great need or trouble. If he actually shows a casual or calloused attitude at such times there is no way that he can win completely the respect of those neglected. On the other hand, the wise pastor knows that people can be reached during hours of trouble who cannot be reached when things are going well. Many people grow spiritually by leaps when they go through crises with the ministry of an understanding and faithful pastor. Furthermore, unchristian members of families in which there has been a crisis are often reached by the church through faithful ministry in the hours of trouble.

An enlarging number of pastors, even in the smaller churches, are seeing the need for an organized plan of pastoral counseling. Most pastors, quite naturally, do most of their counseling in their ministry of crises and stress situations and in their regular or routine calling. In many instances, however, personal needs are not expressed at such times, particularly the latter, and there are people who wish to go alone to counsel with their pastor in the quiet of his study. To meet such needs pastors, especially in cities, are announcing without fanfare a certain period or periods when they are always in their studies and available for counseling. Normally pastors of smaller churches should not announce regular counseling periods until they have observed a definite need for them.

The requests for counseling interviews represent an end product of a man's total ministry. Many factors of his personality and his work contribute to this part of his calling. His mature bearing, regardless of chronological age, suggests that he knows that it is not abnormal for people to have personal problems. His whole manner of life suggests that he is the type of person who can maintain confidences. His friendly contacts with people personally and in groups establish a basic rapport that helps prepare the way for counseling. His preaching comes to grips with real life situations and his sermons demonstrate that he has an understanding of human nature and some real ability to help people with their personal problems.

Many pastors could revolutionize their total programs of regular or routine pastoral calling overnight if they would adopt a systematic plan of visitation. We use the term, regular pastoral calling, to suggest the periodic calls that the pastor makes on members when he is aware of no special needs. Hit-and-miss work in this area means wasted time, ineffective work, and a guilty conscience. Glen Williamson reports a case study of a pastor of a small church who gave superlative care to his people. Williamson asked the pastor how he carried on his program.

"I care for my members first," he said. "A pastor's biggest job is conserving what he has. Then, any new people represent a gain." He had one hundred thirty-two names on his church roll which were divided into three categories. The first group he called "stand-bys." "These," he said, "are present at nearly every service—they are dependable, spiritual people." In this group there were eighty-two members representing thirty-six homes in which to call. He contended that one pastoral call every four months was sufficient for these stable people, which meant nine calls per month.

The second group he captioned, "on the fringes." In this were included new converts, but more especially the spiritually lean and backslidden. They were people who came to church spasmodically; were not dependable and needed spiritual strength and guidance. This list numbered thirty-eight and represented sixteen homes. "These," he said, "must be given special care or we will lose them. We expect to see many of them revived during our meeting. I call in these homes not less than once a month." This meant sixteen "fringe" calls added to the nine "stand-bys."

He spoke of a third group as "shut-ins." They numbered twelve and represented twelve homes. These he called on every week, making a total of forty-nine calls per month. "You see," he said, "I can take Mondays off and still care for my members with just two calls per day." [7]

The above pastor did more regular calling than is demanded in smaller churches, in view of the multiplicity of pastoral tasks. Numerous pastors, even of smaller churches, plan to call less frequently, perhaps once every two months, on many of the people of the second group, as mentioned above, and once a month on shut-ins. With such a modified system a pastor can care for a church with a constituency of one hundred families by making about nine calls a week, or, by calling two short afternoons each week. In addition to this there are, of course, numerous special calls on the sick and the otherwise needy, besides calls on new contacts and friends of the church.

Careful records are part of the genius of a successful system of calling. A pastor must keep an up-to-date file of his calling constituency if he is to work effectively. He needs to make a record of his calls each day, taking note of the date and any special problems encountered. These notations should be put on the family cards in the file. Moreover, at the end of

[7] Glen Williamson, "The Pastor and His Ministry of Calling," *The Christian Minister* (February, 1954), p. 18.

each month he should check up to see if he has completed his calling for the month. Such a system of planned calling saves a pastor from the confusion and frustrations of a hit-and-miss program and it gives him a hearty sense of achievement.

There must be more person-to-person work in a church than a pastor can do alone. This means that he must challenge his laymen to assist him. There are three important emphases along this line. First, the pastor can lead all of his church officials to see that person-to-person contacts, like pastoral visitation, are an important aspect of the work of many church departments. Lay leaders of adult groups, for instance, should make friendly calls on their group members, particularly those showing a loss of interest. Sunday-school teachers should regard calling on their students and families as an essential and integral part of their work. Secondly, churches may maintain lay calling groups that meet regularly, perhaps once a week, in order to contact families for the church. The members of these clubs frequently call on absentees of the Sunday school and church, and they go to new families that have been contacted by the pastor and by members. Thirdly, churches sometimes assign families to certain mature Christians, perhaps Christian couples, who carry on a systematic plan of friendly visitation. This plan may be implemented in many ways. One good example is by the "undershepherd plan." Two representative members are chosen to look after the spiritual and social welfare of others in their neighborhoods.

The office of the Christian pastor is unique. It is a distinct and peculiar creation that involves the loving care and shepherding of souls by a man who has genuine concern for people. A profession embodying the ideals of the Christian pastor is alien to every other faith excepting Christianity.[*]

The pastoral ministry is a creation of Jesus Christ himself.

---

[*] Kenneth S. Latourette, *Missions Tomorrow* (New York: Harper and Brothers, 1936), p. 176.

Before he came the world knew priests, prophets and teachers but not pastors. He not only inaugurated the person-to-person ministry but he brought priestly, prophetic and teaching functions under the control of genuine concern for people. In a superbly fine figure of speech he likened himself to an oriental shepherd of a small flock of sheep who calls his own sheep by name. The sheep also know his voice. This creation of our Lord is timeless and there must be effective pastoral services if there are to be spiritually dynamic churches.

The minister, however, has no monopoly on the basic qualities for an effective person-to-person work. Every Christian worker must exemplify these if he is to serve effectively. The Sunday-school superintendent must be person-minded as well as program-minded. The leader of youth must have the ability to see life through youthful eyes, as well as adult, if he is to influence the young people. The Sunday-school teacher must have genuine love for her students if she is to win them. All church workers must have patience for the long and hard pull.

12 Worshiping in the Smaller Church

"The character of their worship services is the most important factor that has contributed to the growth of some of our smaller churches," said a district superintendent as he accounted for the success of certain rapidly growing smaller congregations in his area. This superintendent, serving a district on the Atlantic seaboard, emphasized that these little churches were not trying "to fight in Saul's armor." They had creatively adapted worship to their own needs with a healthful nonchalance as to how things were done in great metropolitan congregations. This leader said that most of the smaller congregations in his district were holding uniquely effective worship services that had a hearty appeal to unchurched people.

The basic requirements of effective corporate worship are the same, of course, for congregations of all sizes. Worship services must have favorable conditions, meaningful materials, a prepared leadership, and the presence of the Holy Spirit. The same basic results are achieved normally in the personal lives of the worshipers when these requirements are met, whether in a smaller or large church. There are three of these basic results.

First, worship gives persons insight into the will of God. Secondly, worship leads people to commit themselves personally to God's revealed will. Such a commitment may be the sinner's dedication of his life to Christ at the time of his repentance or the Christian's further response to God's will for him. Thirdly, worship provides continuing strength to the dedicated man as he leaves the sanctuary to perform the will of God.

While the basic requirements and results are the same for all worshiping congregations, the smaller church faces some unique problems in getting favorable conditions for its services. It also has some special needs in worship that grow out of its diminutive size. This chapter surveys some of the unique problems and emphases in the worship of smaller congregations.

Securing Proper Conditions for Worship

Smaller churches often encounter difficult problems of worship in the physical limitations of their sanctuaries. Hundreds of congregations worship in small, one room structures that are severely barren and lacking in architectural imagination. Moreover, worship is made difficult because the sancturary is used frequently for Sunday-school and youth activities immediately before worship services. There are also other persistent problems that plague smaller worshiping groups.

Smaller congregations are realizing increasingly that there are many little improvements that can be made so that their sanctuaries may be more worshipful. People in all small churches should be alert along these lines and effect changes that make their church houses suitable places to meet God.

The fact that most small church sanctuaries are used for Sunday school constitutes a more serious problem. If worship follows Sunday school immediately this means that a school must be changed quickly into a sanctuary. Such a matter usually occasions the putting away of Sunday-school materials with dispatch and a minimum of confusion. Sunday-school equipment such as blackboards and flannelgraphs distract worshipers if left in the sanctuary.

A sorely tempted man went to his church for the morning worship service to find a sketch of the devil drawn on a blackboard that had been set back in the corner of the sanctuary during the intermission between Sunday school and morning worship. The devil on the blackboard leered at the congregation with an impish grin as the people sang the great hymns of their faith. He kept on grinning as the pastor preached on "Overcoming Evil" and much of the influence of the sermon was lost. The hard pressed worshiper learned after the benediction that the Sunday-school superintendent, an amateurish cartoonist, had drawn Satan to show the boys and girls how he looks when they do wrong.

Some little churches encounter a difficult problem in having effective worship because many of their people arrive late at the services. Punctuality is especially important in the smaller congregation. Every worshiper is needed at the opening moment and, furthermore, the service is hindered, quite naturally, by the distraction that is occasioned by the arrival of late comers. Many people regard tardiness at the worship service as irreverence toward God much like the discourtesy of being late for an appointment with an important person.

The matter of punctuality is so urgently important that every pastor who has the problem ought to learn why certain ones of his congregation are habitually late. Upon observation he will conclude probably that people go late to church for one of three reasons. First, some people's habits are poorly systematized and they are generally late for all kinds of appointments. Secondly, the late-comers frequently do not realize the importance of religious punctuality. Perhaps they have never understood clearly that tardiness at worship tends to nullify their Christian witness and hinder the service for others. Thirdly, some people have little expectation of meeting God in the early part of the meeting. This attitude indicates spiritual dullness on the part of the worshiper, or, on the other hand, it may be a just incrimination of the service. If the minister considers the early part of the meeting as "preliminary" to something else, perhaps his sermon, then the late-comer is partially right in regarding the first few minutes as unimportant.

Knowing the factors that motivate tardiness in his congregation, the effective pastor plans creative and remedial action. Such a plan usually has two elements. First, the pastor further trains his people in the meaning and nature of corporate worship, and, secondly, he makes certain that every part of the worship service is spiritually vital.

Some churches frequently encounter another difficult problem in the lack of reverence that is shown by the people in the house of God. Sometimes there is general conversation before the service starts and even during the prelude at the actual beginning of the worship. There are some unique reasons for the lack of reverence in small groups. The people often know each other so intimately that they are tempted to chatter at every opportunity. They frequently feel like "one big family" and they have a tendency to express the informality of such intimacy even in the house of God. They do not have the inhibitions that most people experience in the presence of strangers and in large groups.

In addition to fundamental training in the meaning and importance of worship some pastors employ little techniques to help solve this problem. Many have used a "quiet moment" before the call to worship. With this plan the pastor goes to the pulpit a few moments before time for the regular service to start. He arises and stands before the pulpit as a sign of the time for quietness. This method does not represent the use of silence in worship but more properly the use of silence as a preparation for worship.

Rockwell Smith suggests that a short period of personal devotions be held immediately before the start of the worship service. In such a case all of the people join quietly in prayer for some special need represented in the congregation, e. g., a member who is hospitalized or ill at home, young people going away to college, or the success of a series of evangelistic meetings. The special subject of prayer may be announced by the pastor or printed at the top of the order of worship in the bulletin.[1]

---

[1] Rockwell C. Smith, *Rural Church Administration* (Nashville: Abingdon-Cokesbury, 1953), pp. 93, 94.

Smaller congregations are faced also with the problem of the babies crying in the worship service. Some of the parents, perhaps because of the informality that inheres in little groups, are slow to take fretful children out of the meeting. In many cases little churches, needing all of their people at worship, have laid the foundation for such a situation by urging parents of young children to attend regularly and then failing to provide nurseries for the small children.

I have heard a few ministers undertake to solve this problem by telling the mothers not to be concerned about the crying of their babies. In a statement that was meant evidently to suggest superior manly strength these preachers have said, "I can talk louder than the babies can cry." Such a suggestion misses the point entirely. We know that such preachers can take care of themselves while they are in the pulpit. Crying babies may not distract them because they are deeply engrossed in the content of their messages but their listeners are distracted. A crying baby, lovely and innocent as it is, can nullify the pastor's whole week of sermon preparation.

The nursery is the best answer to this problem. Whole families should be urged to attend church. If a mother ever needs the strength that comes from worship it is when her children are small. The church should thus provide for whole family attendance. This will mean that provision will have to be made for the care of the smallest children. There are three principles that are basic for a successful church nursery. First, the nursery must be equipped to give comfort and protection to the children. Secondly, it must have a competent person in charge. Thirdly, the presentation of the nursery care must be made in such a way that parents do not feel that their children are "rejected" from the service.

The proper seating of the people in the house of God is another important condition for effective worship. This is a task for the ushers. Their work is important even in the smallest congregation with large sanctuaries. In such situations the people, without ushers, usually occupy the back seats leaving a cavern between the preacher and themselves. If they do not do this they are likely to scatter themselves over the church like farmhouses on a countryside. Ushers seat the people in a group at the front of the church, even though there are only a few in a spacious room. This aids in every part of the meeting. The people participate as a group and the preacher is thus inspired in his preaching.

Every worshiper should remember that a local congregation gives a corporate testimony to its community. A church becomes known in its neighborhood for its acts of reverence or irreverence. All of the matters mentioned in this section enter into the corporate testimony of a church and they enhance or diminish its opportunities in the community. Lack of punctuality on the part of worshipers suggests apathetic and unconcerned attitudes to the outside people who are present. All acts of disorder and confusion suggest a lack of devotion or, worse still, bad manners. Sitting in the back seats, unless there are valid reasons, proclaims loudly that people are either apologetic for or disinterested in their church.

Singing in Smaller Congregations

The music of a smaller congregation can be attractive and effective if it first faces realistically its limitations and then plans its music around its resources. Sometimes churches, both small and larger, are unwilling to accept their limitations with the result that they undertake to do things beyond their abilities. Little churches find that their primary resources in music are in congregational singing.

Congregational singing is the music *par excellence* in Christian history. Jesus and his disciples sang a hymn, perhaps the *Hallel,* as our Lord faced the cross (Matthew 26:30). The earliest Christians emphasized congregational singing by use of hymns and spiritual songs (Colossians 3:16; Ephesians 5:19; I Corinthians 14:26). One of Luther's famous Ninety-five

Theses demanded that the Roman Catholic Church restore congregational singing to the people. The Protestant Reformation gave much attention to the promotion of hymn singing. Coleridge said that Martin Luther did as much for the Reformation by his hymns as he did by the translation of the Bible.[2] The Wesleyan revival was distinguished by the hymn singing of the early Methodists. Vincent, an eighteenth century rector of the Church of England, exclaimed, "Where one person has been won away from the established church by the preaching of the Wesleyans, ten have been won away by their singing."[3] It appears historically that every great evangelistic movement has been borne along on the wings of melody and song. This observation is attested by contemporary revival movements that are characterized by the hearty singing of the people.

There must be careful planning and preparation for congregational singing if it is to be a source of inspiration and power. H. Augustine Smith once said, "Of all the fine arts in the service of the church, congregational singing, big brother of them all, receives scant attention."[4] This is frequently true, especially in smaller congregations. Little churches must meet three conditions if their congregational singing is to be worshipful and effective. First, they must provide for effective leadership. Such may be furnished by the pastor or song leader, or if no person is capable of song leadership an effective organist or pianist can set the tempo for good singing. New hymns should be learned in practice periods that may be held in periodical hymn singing meetings, in Sunday school, in the early part of the evening service, at the midweek meeting, or at any other convenient time. The song leader, if qualified, conducts these singing periods. If no leader in the church is available, a director of music from a neighboring church can often be

---

[2] Cf. E. E. Harper, *Church Music and Worship* (New York: 1924), p. 34.

[3] *Ibid.*, p. 46.

[4] *Ibid.*, p. 9.

secured. Thirdly, a careful selection of hymns for worship should be made by the pastor and other worship leaders. Many congregations use a small variety of hymns in their services. A few years ago, E. E. Harper stated to a group of pastors that the average church uses no more than twenty-five hymns during a year in its Sunday morning and evening services. Some of the preachers present challenged the statement but upon examination a few of them found that the speaker had actually understated their cases. A pastor of a large congregation discovered, much to his consternation, that he had selected only fifteen different hymns for his services during the past year.[5]

Many smaller churches rely too heavily on choirs and they thus neglect congregational singing. There are two reasons why this is done. Little congregations often imitate large churches with the assumption that a choir is necessary for effective worship. Secondly, smaller churches often over-emphasize the importance of choir singing, along with Protestantism generally, because of a "spectator" attitude that has been fostered by radio, television and other forms of entertainment.

If a smaller congregation is to have a choir it should be able to meet the two requirements for good choral music. There must be a conductor, in the first place, who has the training, Christian character and time to perform his task successfully. Then, there must be a sufficiently large number of capable singers, consistently Christian, who can devote enough time in preparing for choral music.

I recently preached in a small church that lacked both of these essentials. The "choir" stumbled through the hymns as badly as did the congregation and it struggled through the anthem with the result that it distracted from worship. The group had no director and it was obvious that it had spent little time in practice. This "choir" was not really a group of singers

---

[5] *Ibid.*, pp. 120, 121.

but rather a group of people who had accepted the special recognition the church afforded them by permitting them to sit in the choir seats.

There is a serious hazard, however, for the smaller church in the selection of the best singers for the choir. This often so impoverishes the congregation of capable and willing singers that the congregational singing is lethargic and lifeless. It is surely a mistake to have the choir do most of the singing. Few things deaden a worship service as readily as listless singing by the people themselves. This often results in churches that have depleted their congregations of their best singers.

In many cases smaller churches find it better to use smaller singing groups. Mixed quartets or trios offer a focal center and leadership in congregational singing as well as contribute generously in special music. In some instances a capable soloist may be relied upon for the special singing. It is more worshipful to hear the gospel sung simply and sincerely by a small group or a soloist than by an ill prepared choir that undertakes to sing something beyond its reach.

The Primacy of Preaching

Broadly speaking, there are two types of Christian worship, the liturgical and the free. Liturgical worship is found in the Roman Catholic Church and in a few of the older denominations of Protestantism. There is presently, however, a strong trend toward the use of liturgy in many of the major Protestant churches. Free worship is found in most of the newer and more evangelistic churches of American Christianity.

Liturgical worship centers around the priestly, and free worship centers around the prophetic. In the former the minister as priest leads the congregation in worship that emphasizes ceremonial forms, religious symbols and formal prayers. In free worship the minister as prophet declares the Word and the will of God to the people. The sermon serves as the focal center and it is indeed often the high point of the service. Liturgical worship is oriented in traditional materials but free worship takes these materials, especially the Scripture, and relates them to the present situation. Free worship emphasizes thought and instruction instead of the sensuous appeal of the symbolic object and act. It is likewise less rigidly ordered and has a place for greater freedom and spontaneity on the part of both minister and lay worshipers.

Most smaller congregations need to have free worship because they must grow or perish. Free worship has virile evangelistic elements that attract outsiders and often bring about their conversion. This type of worship does not mean that every service must be revivalistic but the worship of the smaller church generally should have an evangelistic motif. The value of free worship as a means of evangelism is attested in the fact that many of the larger denominations in American Protestantism were built with the type of worship that was simple and free.

Most of the unchurched people respond more heartily to worship that is simple and free, though well ordered, than to the services that are formal and liturgical. There are three reasons for this.

First, most of the unchurched people respond more favorably to free worship because our culture has conditioned them to informality in groups. We are educated in class rooms that are informal with a generous interchange of ideas. Most of our business and professional contacts are informal. Men go to a business or professional conference and find themselves calling each other by their first names almost immediately after they have been introduced. Many of their discussions and business sessions are highly informal. Radio and television programs confirm free and informal attitudes. A continuous conditioning in free and informal meetings such as is found generally in American society causes people to feel ill at ease in highly formal and rigidly ordered meetings.

Secondly, and more important, unchurched people normally

appreciate worship that is free and informal because of their simple religious orientation. The unchurched people are generally unlearned in a religious vocabulary and uninstructed in the meaning of ceremonies. They do not grasp the significance of rites and symbols inasmuch as they have not been trained in their use. Likewise they have not developed the sentiments that are necessary for an appreciation of symbolic forms of worship. This suggests that elaborate worship means little to them. Putting an unchurched man in an elaborate worship service is comparable to putting a boy who is a high school freshman in a graduate school with a class of Ph.D. candidates. Like the boy, the unchurched man often doesn't know what it is all about. Liturgical worship assumes a far more extensive religious education and experience on the part of worshipers than unchurched people have.

This point is illustrated by the preference of hymns on the part of the common man, both within and without the church. What kind of hymns does the average person prefer? The surveys show that the grand stately hymns of the church are not first choice with the populace. Recently a radio program in California took a survey. There were ten thousand replies from people of many denominations and from many who were outside of the church. The top favorite was "The Old Rugged Cross" by a wide margin. Then in order were the following, "The Love of God," "In the Garden," "What a Friend We Have in Jesus," "Beyond the Sunset," "Precious Lord, Take My Hand," "Rock of Ages," "It's No Secret," "Abide With Me," and "No One Cares for Me Like Jesus." All of these hymns, with the possible exception of two, both of which are rated low, are really gospel songs that are unsuitable for liturgical worship but are fitted for free and informal services.

It may be objected that this list was strongly influenced by the character of the radio program that carried out the survey. This may have some truth in it but as noted by the former editor of *The Christian Century,* hardly a revivalist, the list is too much like other lists for the objection to be really convincing.[6]

A district superintendent of a major denomination in the Middle West gives a graphic illustration of the evangelistic outreach of simplified worship. In a small city there were five local churches of his denomination. One of these churches, once strong, was at the point of closing. A new pastor was appointed in an effort to save the church. The pastor broadened the church's appeal to the common man by simplifying its worship. Congregational singing was emphasized, preaching was restored to its central place, and many of the litanies were omitted. Within three years' time that church, recently threatened with closing, was having the largest congregations of any of the five churches of its denomination in the city.

Thirdly, and most important, free worship, as an agency of the Holy Spirit, convicts men of their sins because it gives a central place to the preacher who takes eternal truth and applies it specifically to present conditions. Free worship emphasizes the sermon while liturgical worship, as stated above, exalts traditional forms, prayers and symbols. Paul did not misunderstand his commission when he subordinated the symbolic ordinance to the evangelical proclamation. "For Christ sent me not to baptize but to preach the gospel" (I Corinthians 1:17). The preacher as a prophet stands at the center of free worship and the high moments come when he declares specifically God's eternal truth for the present moment and when he, as a shepherd-priest, prays for his people in highly relevant petitions. Such worship has convicting power. This results in conversions and the growth of the church.

Liturgical worship, on the other hand, puts the priest in the center. Priests are servants of tradition, being more interested in the past than in the present. They have great appreciation

[6] "What Are America's Favorite Hymns?" *The Christian Century*, (September 16, 1953), p. 1044.

for properly patterned forms but often little interest in the pressing contemporary problems that plague man. Gaius Glenn Atkins suggests that the priests' excessive dependence upon symbols may actually be due to his lack of a strong intellectual hold upon religious reality.[7]

It should be re-emphasized that the rites of elaborate worship are often in a lofty religious vocabulary that does not grip people in a workaday world. Sometimes the cutting edge of their words has been dulled by frequent and undefined use. How often have traditional words become equivocal and powerless to confront men with their sins. Great historical statements, once throbbing with spiritual energy, often are powerless in another day because of a lack of definition. Equivocal words and concepts have occasioned a tremendous loss of vigor in today's religious world. Thousands of people use sanctimonious words but appear to be unaffected by them.

Any man might go to a dozen churches, even in a smaller city, on a Sunday morning and hear large congregations "grievously confess" their "sins" to God in corporate penitential litanies. After the service, however, most of the people casually resume the sins they had confessed. Here is the use of sanctimonious words without action. I am sure that the hour of 11:00 a.m. to 12:00 noon on Sunday mornings must be a weary one to God as he listens to vast congregations confess sins that they cherish. I hear the Almighty saying, "I am weary of verbal repentance." How can we expect sinners to be convicted of their sins in a liturgical service when professing Christians themselves do not mend their own iniquitous ways?

The prophet, champion of rugged and unadorned truth, has always driven the priest, his antagonist, from the field when it comes to soul saving. "The periods of decadence (in the church) have been marked by the loss of the power of the pulpit; and the eras of revival and reform have been heralded by

[7] Gaius Glenn Atkins, *Preaching and the Mind of Today* (New York: Round Table, 1934), pp. 27, 28.

a renewal of the preacher's influence." [8] Philip Schaff, prince among church historians, says, "It is living Christianity proclaimed by living preachers that has always been, and will be to the end of time, the great missionary agency." [9]

There are reasons why the prophet, as preacher, convicts men of sins. He speaks personally, "Ye have robbed God" (Malachi 3:8, 9). He deliberately confronts the hypocrites and the evils of his age (Matthew 3:7-10). He defines his terms and restores the cutting edge to words because he wishes, above all else, to be understood clearly (Matthew 11:1-15). He has no interest in hollow forms and he condemns the use of empty and sanctimonious words (Isaiah 1:10-15; cf. Luke 6:46). His aim is to convict and he wishes actions and not words only.

A few years ago a noted Catholic, W. E. Orchard, acknowledged the inability of liturgical worship to reach outsiders. This man, in the highest of liturgical traditions, pleaded for informal Sunday evening services in Catholic churches. He wanted the sermon featured so that non-Catholics might be reached.

> How unless through preaching are we going to reach the outsider? Books and pamphlets, necessary and effective as they may be, will not take the place of the spoken word with its note of conviction. . . . The people will always be attracted by preaching; they will always come where it is good; and preaching has been and always will be the great converting agency, whether from sin or unbelief. [10]

We need a whole new race of prophets. Our religious words have lost their power. Our liturgies are making people

[8] Alfred E. Garvie, *The Christian Preacher* (New York: Scribner's, 1921), p. 3.

[9] Philip Schaff, *Theological Propaedeutic* (New York: Scribner's, 1893), p. 474.

[10] W. E. Orchard, "The Place of Preaching in the Catholic Church," *The Catholic World* (April, 1941), p. 49.

religious but not transformed. America is having a so-called revival of religion but also a decrease in ethics and morals. An evangelist friend told me recently that he had just talked to a recovered alcoholic at a camp meeting at which he had been preaching. The recovered alcoholic, religious in his way, took God's name in vain as he told the evangelist how the Almighty had delivered him from his drink. Such a coalescence of the sinful and the supposed sacred is not singular today. Whole congregations have united the sacred and the secular in a quasi-Christian religion because the words of the prophet have not been heard.

Advancing Through Christian Education

13

Many smaller churches find their best opportunities for advance through Christian Education activities, broadly called the Church school. These activities include the Sunday school, children's groups, young people's work, daily vacation Bible schools, weekday Bible schools, adult educational programs, and many others. The church school is the spearhead of the smaller church in its crusade for souls. Church leaders, both ministerial and lay, who are not alert to the opportunities it provides are among those who walk with the blind.

Outreach Through Christian Education

The Sunday school, as a part of the church school, has a unique capacity to extend the outreach of the church because of its wide appeal. It has a large variety of activities that are graded for people from beginners to the older aged. There are activities that charm and delight the three year olds and there are Bible study and discussion groups to challenge the older people, even those who are the most philosophical and profound. The Sunday school appeals to all of the people in a manner in which no other church organization can.

The present-day revival of interest in religion has strengthened the appeal of the Sunday school and other Christian education activities. People are realizing increasingly that religious knowledge is desirable and important. Religious illiteracy is now old fashioned. The awakened interest in religion increases the willingness and desire of parents to have their children in Sunday school. It also aids in the recruitment of adults, especially younger parents, for Sunday school and other church activities. Some smaller churches find one of their best evangelistic opportunities in classes of young parents who bring their children to Sunday school.

The present interest in religion, however, does not suggest that Sunday schools will now grow automatically. Unlike Topsy, no Sunday school grows up by itself. Even an attractive and effective Sunday-to-Sunday program will not assure growth unless there are plans and means of outreach into the community.

Sunday schools must be organized for advance. There must be vision and planning for expansion. There must be ways of reaching the unchurched people in the community. Strange as it may seem, many Sunday schools with good programs have not developed means of outreach. They are organized only for holding operations. They are set up only to maintain the *status quo*. There are several things that can be done in organizing a Sunday school for advance and outreach.

First, every teacher ought to be a Sunday-school promoter —an enthusiastic salesman for the school. Effective teachers are alert to opportunities to recruit new members for their classes and for the school as a whole. They assume responsibility also for contacting personally their own absentees. They, furthermore, inspire enthusiasm, like a capable sales manager, in their class members to invite and bring their friends to the Sunday school.

Second, every effective Sunday school should have a secretary whose work is to make lists of the absentees each Sunday. This work is done sometimes by the regular secretary of the Sunday school and at other times by a person elected specifically to that work. The secretary of absentees takes responsibility for seeing that those who miss Sunday school are contacted. Sometimes she sends an appropriate card to them. At other times she gives lists of absentees to teachers, the calling committee, or the pastor who, in each case, follow up the students who were not present. The work of identifying and contacting the absentees is most important in view of the fact that the average Sunday school has only about two-thirds of its students present each Sunday. An effective method of contacting absent people is a *must* in an effective and growing Sunday school.

Third, a group of lay visitors is of inestimable value to the church that is trying seriously to extend its outreach into its community. Such a group of lay people, both men and women, meet regularly each week on a specified night and make contacts for the Sunday school and for the church. They call on the people who have been absent. They also call on non-attendants of the Sunday school and church by using the church's responsibility or prospect list. Such an evening of calling demands careful preparation. Some person, usually the pastor, prepares lists of persons upon whom each team is to call.

Fourth, for most effective outreach and growth, the whole Sunday school must become an enthusiastic group about its program and possibilities. A church school has no place for spectators; every person, with the possible exception of the youngest children, should be a participant in increasing the outreach into the community. Such a situation arises out of a high morale that is based on a recognition of purposes, an effective program and a sense of mission. It is fostered further by the announcement of specific goals and the use of specific methods in enlisting people to attend.

All of the families having children and youth in the Sunday school should be accepted genuinely in the church's broad constituency. They should receive announcements of the church activities. Sunday-school teachers, as well as the pastor, should call on them. A spiritual ministry should be provided for them, especially if they are not active members of another church. Some Sunday schools encourage the teachers to have informal teas for the mothers of the children in their classes. This provides a favorable time to discuss the work of the class and to give a Christian witness. A friendly attitude should be shown to parents of church school children at the time of Special Day programs. The families of the Sunday-school children should also be included in some of the fellowship dinners of the church where the warmth of Christian friendship can get hold of their hearts and draw them closer to the church. Most families, though ostensibly casual about religion, appreciate the sincere interest of the church.

The growing Sunday school provides the smaller church with its best evangelistic field. No church can wish for a better one. It is not a field *at* its doors but *within* its doors. This is true because many of the children in the average Sunday school are not converted. J. N. Barnette, of the Sunday-school department of the Southern Baptist Convention, estimates the percentages of unconverted students in the various departments as follows: seventy-five percent of the Juniors, forty-five percent of the Intermediates, fifteen percent of the young people, and eight percent of the adults.[1] The evangelistic opportunity of the Sunday school is seen also in the fact that children and youth are sensitive to the call of Christ. Most Christians are converted before the age of twenty-five years. The golden harvest years for the church are in early and middle adolescence. The Sunday school and other Christian education activities in the total church school touch large numbers of children and youth at the time when they are likely to respond to the evangelistic challenge. Again, the Sunday school offers many smaller churches their best evangelistic fields because of the variety of its appeals and opportunities. There is the evangelistic appeal of worship, e. g., in decision days and special evangelistic periods. There is the appeal of the study of the Bible. Furthermore, smaller groups of children and youth in classes that are informal provide a good situation for students to yield to Christ. Teachers have an unusual opportunity to

[1] J. N. Barnette, *The Place of The Sunday School in Evangelism* (Nashville: Sunday School Board of the Southern Baptist Convention, 1949), pp. 28, 29.

personally witness to their students and urge them to commit their lives to Christ. There is also an evangelistic appeal in the social activities as Christian friends witness to others by the quality of their lives and by their words. There is, moreover, an evangelistic appeal in the challenge to service which is often made in Sunday schools.

Sunday schools must be organized for evangelistic success if there are to be conversions. A promising field does not assure a bountiful harvest. The grain must be gathered in. There are three essential elements in successful evangelistic work in the church schools of smaller churches.

First, the pastor is the key man in developing an evangelistic spirit in all of the Christian education activities. He sets the evangelistic tone. He shares his vision with his people. He inspires all of the leaders and workers to make the evangelistic motif central in their work. He leads in the matter of outlining the evangelistic strategy of the whole church school. He keeps the evangelistic concern before the people in his messages, his pastoral work, in his board meetings, and in the workers' conferences. Moreover, soul winning pastors frequently give short evangelistic messages to the whole Sunday school and appeal for genuine commitments to Christ. Sometimes they go to the various departments and classes and speak informally to the children and youth about serving the Lord. Evangelistic pastors promote plans that are designed to develop the soul winning qualities of all officers, leaders and teachers in the whole program of Christian education. They also help plan special evangelistic meetings for children and youth.

Second, the teachers are the main line of evangelistic advance in the Sunday school. They are God's evangels to their classes. If this line fails there will be severe losses; if it succeeds, there will be gains. Thousands of adults have been lost forever to the church because some Sunday-school teachers failed in their work. Contrariwise, thousands are now in the church because certain devoted and concerned teachers appealed to their students to serve Christ. More than anyone else in the Sunday school, the teacher stands in the pivotal position to win children and youth to the Lord. The eternal destinies of many boys and girls are in their hands.

Sunday-school teachers should keep the evangelistic appeal uppermost in all of their work. It is not enough to transmit a body of religious knowledge to the students. One can know a great deal about the Bible and still be a sinner—perhaps a more astute one because of his religious orientation. Something must happen in the lives of the class members. That teacher has failed ultimately in his work if he does not see the lives of his students transformed by God's power.

Sunday-school teachers should witness personally to their students. Some fail to do this because of timidity, believing that they would embarrass their students by speaking to them about their relationship to Christ. The situation is usually otherwise. It is the teacher who is embarrassed. Many boys and girls expect and want their teachers to talk naturally to them about their relationship to God.

Teachers must be trained in the soul winning emphasis because evangelistic teaching and witnessing are an art. A number of factors contribute to the development of this splendid art. It is indeed rooted in the devotional and spiritual life of the teacher. Genuine spiritual concern and passion lay the foundation for soul winning interest. Furthermore, the evangelistic tone and emphasis of the Sunday school do much to foster soul winning teaching. The evangelistic emphasis is usually found in churches that expect to have converts. Finally, actual instruction in evangelistic teaching is invaluable. There are basic principles that underlie this art as is the case with all other arts. These principles should be comprehended and put into practice. The Sunday school and leadership training departments in most denominations have courses that relate to this matter.

Third, special plans should be made for the conversion of children and youth. Their conversion is so important that this matter must not be left to casual or perfunctory measures. Churches should provide their children and younger people the best possible evangelistic advantages. The Sunday school should organize to have its members in services of the regular revival meetings. Certain nights of revivals may be designated for specific classes or for the Sunday school as a whole. In some cases the same end is achieved by the promotion of family nights. Some churches have found it helpful to promote late afternoon meetings after school for the smaller children. Many churches have used daily vacation Bible schools and weekday Bible schools with outstanding evangelistic results.

Conserving the Results

The genuine conversion of Sunday-school members is a significant achievement in any church. It should be remembered, however, that conversion is only the beginning of the Christian life. Converts need nurture and guidance, especially in the earliest days. From the standpoint of local church advancement, many smaller churches would show phenomenal growth in attendance and membership if they were to inaugurate an effective program of convert culture.

Christian education activities, comprising the church school, are uniquely qualified to supply Christian nurture. The church school provides nurture to converts by *instruction*. It lays primary emphasis upon teaching the Bible but deals also with principles of Christian living, Christian beliefs, the history of the Christian church and the denomination, local church organization, and other important areas of religious knowledge.

It is imperative today that the church take seriously its mission of teaching. Other institutions including public schools, community groups, and many families are highly secularized and provide little religious instruction. Youth will remain untaught religiously if the church fails in its mission and converts will fail in the Christian life if they remain uninstructed.

Teaching must be personalized if it is to be of maximum

helpfulness in Christian living. It must have a hearty life-situation emphasis. It must be related to actual living. A former president of Harvard University emphasized the word "relevance" as his educational keyword. He knew that unrelated bits of knowledge were of minor value. Every church school teacher and leader should keep in mind the idea of relevance. Even the Bible may be taught academically, as an end in itself, but have little relevance to Christian experience. The Bible must be taught as the textbook of life. Its eternal principles of righteousness should be discussed in contemporary terms. The problems of its characters, real men and women, should be related to contemporary living. Present, everyday problems should be solved in the light of the Word.

There are many effective ways of providing systematic instruction to younger Christians. Perhaps the most basic is in the Sunday-school class. In addition to this some pastors spend short periods, perhaps twenty minutes, in the various departments giving instruction in Christian living. At other times, instruction is given in other groups that meet regularly on Sunday evening or during the week. Midweek prayer meetings have become often a time of convert culture, on the assumption that many of the older Christians need the same spiritual menu. Many pastors have organized special classes for converts. Arthur C. Archibald recommends that every church have a school for Christian living.[2] This school should be held once a year with the classes meeting one night per week for six or seven successive weeks. The classes should be graded and they should study relevant materials. Many of the denominations have study courses prepared. Archibald believes that such annual schools should enroll normally about one-half of the congregation.

The church school provides nurture to converts through *worship*. Christian education activities are equipped superbly to

[2] Arthur C. Archibald, *Establishing the Converts* (Philadelphia: The Judson Press, 1952), pp. 57, 58.

do this. They can provide a sort of tailor-made type of worship for their members inasmuch as the groups are usually small, highly informal and highly personal. Christian education groups are usually more homogeneous than a worshiping congregation on Sunday morning. There is also more personal participation generally in the worshiping groups of the church school. All of these factors make worship increasingly alive and meaningful to the participants.

The Sunday school should promote Sunday morning worship attendance, either in the regular worship service or in a special junior worship service. George Truett once said that the saddest parade in all the world is the parade of Sunday-school children that marches from the church to their homes just as the church service is beginning. This parade that leaves the church each Sunday at 11 : 00 a.m. symbolizes the church's failure to take seriously its mission of soul winning and Christian nurture.

It is best, normally, for the smaller church to have the children in the regular worship service, especially those of junior age and above. This demands that the service be of such a character to enable all, both younger and older, to worship God together. Wise pastors have always made sure that there were interests and emphases for both younger and older members of the congregations. Some pastors, in ministering to the group as a whole, have delivered a short children's sermon in the early part of the worship service and then later have preached a sermon designed primarily for adults. It is probably better, however, to minister to the whole congregation throughout the entire service than to have worshipers "getting on and off" at the various "amens."

The church fosters Christian growth in converts by *fellowship*. Membership in small groups, such as Sunday-school classes or boys' or girls' clubs, is often a highly meaningful thing in the lives of children. In such groups, the members have a clear sense of belonging. There is a genuine mutuality and comradeship among all. The standards of the group are accepted and the ideals become contagious. All of the group members join heartily in carrying out the program. Such factors provide a situation *par excellence* for spiritual growth when the group is itself sincerely Christian.

Christian fellowship is uniquely important in the lives of young people. Perhaps at no other period in life do people wish more for Christian comradeship. When separated from a Christian group, converted young people often feel alone and rejected because of their Christian principles. They are on hazardous grounds when this happens. On the other hand, the spiritual lives of young people flourish in situations of Christian association. Spiritual values become increasingly attractive when seen in esteemed friends. Christian principles become confirmed personally when demonstrated by associates. The frown of the world is less forbidding when in the company of Christian friends. The organization and maintenance of an active young people's group is a matter of the highest importance for even the smallest churches.

The church school fosters Christian growth in converts through *Christian service*. This is also a matter of great importance. Without it, converts frequently fail in their new life or they become passive and quiescent believers. With opportunities to serve, younger Christians are likely to become productive and effective in the work of the church. The present emphasis on numbers and the contemporary interest in quick and easy methods of developing Christians—often only respectable church members—have caused some leaders to neglect Christian service as a method of spiritual nurture. Sunday-school teachers, for instance, find it easier to talk twenty minutes to their classes than to inaugurate and supervise a successful service project that utilizes all of the class members.

Jesus gave us the pattern in this matter. On some occasions his first words to new believers were a commission to perform a task. He emphasized the performance of practical service in the spiritual development and training of his disciples. His pattern is timeless. Today, service activities ought to be an important part of the curriculum of every Christian education group. Such activities offer an opportunity for an implementation of the principles taught in the classes and they foster Christian development in an outstanding manner, especially in youth and adults.

The church's opportunities have never been greater along this line. There has never been a time when there were so many ways to express the gospel and so many means to advance the Kingdom of God. There is a Christian task for everyone, no matter how unique his abilities, and he needs to perform that task for the saving of his own soul.

Christian education is one of the basic ways by which churches can fulfill the great commission. The church school activities are pre-eminently important in "the making of disciples" and they are essential in the matter of "teaching them to observe all things."

14 Advancing Through Evangelism

The formula for evangelistic success in a local church is like a doctor's prescription. It contains a number of elements that are correctly compounded. A church cannot be effective by using only one method of soul winning. Neither can it succeed by emphasizing one method out of proportion to the others. Unlike patent medicine, there is no cure-all for local church evangelism and the formula is surely not the same for every church. It, like the doctor's prescription, must be written in the light of local needs and opportunities.

There are two general principles, however, that apply to all evangelistic churches. First, the whole church must have a genuine concern for the work of saving souls. The evangelistic impulse must be expressed in every department and activity. An evangelical church has no place for a group that has no evangelistic relevance. Second, every day must be a day of evangelism. The work of redeeming souls is not seasonal and no effort should be made to regulate it by the calendar. This does not mean that there will be converts every day. It does mean, however, that every day will be a day of gospel seed sowing. The fruit is harvested whenever it is ready, sometimes regularly through the year and at other times in great revival seasons.

There are two pre-eminently important methods of evangelism that have been validated both by church history and by contemporary Christianity. These are (1) lay witnessing and (2) revivals or evangelistic preaching. These methods are not isolated, standing alone as if each of them were self-sufficient.

In the first place, each of them depends heavily upon the whole church program and, secondly, they themselves are closely related.

Advancing Through Lay Witnessing

Some churches, like individual persons, have agoraphobia. People with this complex have a fear of the out-of-doors. They feel safer in the enclosures of their own homes. It is the same way with churches that keep their gospel contained within four sacred walls.

The matter of taking the gospel to sinners is a great imperative of this goal. Nowhere in the New Testament are sinners commanded to go to church but Christians are commanded to take the gospel to the unconverted. Jesus himself went to those in the highways and byways and he gave us the pattern for all time by organizing his disciples into teams of personal workers and by sending them out to the lost.

The prerequisites for personal witnessing are high. A personal witness must be able, indeed, to tell about his faith but, even more important, he must demonstrate his faith. This calls for effective Christian living in the presence of the people who receive his witness. Apart from victorious personal living, witnessing is largely verbal and often ineffective in the matter of making genuine converts.

The Christian message can never be adequately communicated by words alone because Christianity is *life* and it needs to be demonstrated by actual victorious living. Its very genius is in a transformed life. Christianity is unique among the religions of the world inasmuch as it cannot be communicated simply by speech. The laws of Judaism may be expressed quite adequately by words. The moral codes of Buddhism and Confucianism can be described in speech and writing. The proper worship of liturgical religions may be stated in verbal symbols. In contrast to these, the genius of Christianity must be lived.

On the other hand, a demonstrated faith must be witnessed

to by words. It is right at this point that many smaller evangelical churches fail. They often have large numbers of consistent Christians who are eminently qualified to do personal witnessing, yet these Christians frequently fail to speak about Christ. This is sometimes occasioned by a timidity or a reserve that ought to be overcome. In fairness to these people, it should be noted that it frequently is harder to witness to one's personal faith, sometimes highly intimate, than to talk about what his church is doing. It is also easier to ask for a church membership than it is to talk frankly about another's inner spiritual needs. The fact remains, nevertheless, no matter what the difficulties, that evangelicals are having a tremendous loss of spiritual capital because of an unwarranted reticence on the part of many earnest Christians. This is Protestantism's greatest loss.

Spontaneous personal witnessing is the most effective kind. Happy is that church that has a group of Christians, even though it is small, that talk to others about Christ as enthusiastically and naturally as most people talk about the new car they have bought. It seems that this type of witnessing characterized the apostolic church. All of the believers that were driven from Jerusalem upon the persecution that followed Stephen's death "went everywhere preaching (announcing the word" (Acts 8:4). On an occasion earlier than this, Peter had stated the attitude of every believer, "for we cannot but speak the things which we have seen and heard" (Acts 4:20).

Most of the churches must organize their people for lay evangelistic visitation to assure that it is really done, and done systematically. This whole matter has been discussed extensively in recent literature on evangelism and an extended discussion is not warranted here.[1]

---

[1] The following titles define plans for lay visitation evangelism: Dawson C. Bryan, *A Workable Plan of Evangelism* (New York: Abingdon-Cokesbury, 1945); Eugene A. Golay, *Four Nights for God in the Local Church* (Nashville: Tidings, 1954); George E. Sweazey, *Effective Evangelism* (New York: Harper & Brothers, 1953); Robert E. Coleman, "Organized for Lay Evangelism," *The Christian Minister*, VIII (May, 1956), pp. 3-7.

We shall note briefly seven essential principles of a successful program of lay evangelistic visitation. These principles, like the pillars of a building, are necessary for an effective basis of lay witnessing.

1. The pastor and his committee on evangelism should formulate an effective plan of lay evangelism. Literature on the subject should be studied. Supplies for carrying out the program should be at hand for all the workers.* If the plan is for a four-night campaign the dates should be set well in advance. If the campaign is for a regular week-to-week program the regular time of meeting should be designated.

2. The prospect list of the church should be brought up to date and enlarged. This is sometimes done by a committee on prospects that begins its work several weeks before the actual visitation campaign starts. The name and address of every person for whom the church is responsible is put on the list. The names of unchurched people are included in the church's responsibility. A community canvass should be conducted unless, of course, the names of prospects are available from a recent neighborhood survey.

3. The workers should be selected wisely. It is usually best not to call for volunteers for lay visitation evangelism because frequently unqualified people offer their services. The pastor and his committee on evangelism should select victorious Christian laymen who have a passion to see people converted. These laymen should be able to meet people effectively and they should have an ability to converse persuasively about their faith. Other workers should be selected as prayer warriors, assistants with records and general promoters of the program. Persons who

---

* Non-denominational visitation evangelism materials may be ordered from Tidings, 1908 Grand Avenue, Nashville 5, Tennessee. Tidings has the large turnover charts, *They Went Forth Two by Two*, $12.00; chart booklets, *They Went Forth Two by Two*, 35 cents; the *Visitation Evangelism Packet* that contains all materials that are normally necessary for a program in a church of 100 members, $3.00; and the *Fisherman's Club Packet* that contains materials for promoting a permanent program of visitation evangelism, $1.00.

are not equipped for actual visitation work can be used in other parts of the program.

4. The pastor should train the workers adequately. This is done often in a thirty minute period, frequently from 6:30 to 7:00 p.m., immediately prior to the actual visitation. The training includes the techniques of effective calling, the way to handle difficult situations, and how to get commitments. The turnover chart, *They Went Forth Two by Two,* by Tidings, is very helpful in this training. The Tidings chart booklet by the same title reproduces this material in smaller form. Departments of evangelism usually have helpful denominational materials for orienting laymen in this work. Moreover, many pastors have a good background in this area.

5. The pastor should assign prospects to the visiting teams. Normally, five prospects should be assigned each evening to each team. This number anticipates that the team will actually make about three calls in view of the fact that some people will be away from home. Careful thought should be given to making the assignments in view of such factors as sex, age, personality, and the ability of the visitors.

6. The visitors should report immediately upon their visitation. All workers should return to the church and turn in the cards with their records. Unvisited assignments can then be regrouped and prepared for the next time of visitation. The group of visitors should share their experiences, both victories and problems.

7. The church should make lay visitation a year-round activity. If it starts with a four-night campaign, plans should be made on the last night to continue the program on a regular basis.

Four successive nights of lay evangelism are valuable in making a concentrated drive to cover systematically all the prospects of a church. Such a plan is also valuable in connection with a series of evangelistic meetings. The regular week-to-week plan of visitation helps to sustain a strong evangelistic emphasis continually. Many churches, even smaller ones, should use both plans.

The ultimate purpose of all personal evangelism is to win people to Jesus Christ. It often happens, however, that people are not genuinely converted in a short visit by a couple of laymen. If these people are pressed for an immediate decision, unmoved by the Holy Spirit, they are likely to make a profession of faith without being converted. Such prospects should be related to church departments—the Sunday school, adult groups, youth groups, etc.—and be encouraged to participate actively in all church services. The influence of the church along with continued personal visitation often brings them to a sense of deep spiritual need. This slower way is spiritually valid and it contributes more to the Kingdom than a method of obtaining hasty and spurious professions of faith.

Many smaller evangelical churches should fulfill the great commission by personally seeking out people on "the other side of the tracks." The pastor of a local church in a major denomination states that about all of the middle class and thrifty people of his community have been churched. While there is little evangelistic opportunity among the "nice" people, there are large numbers of poorer folk for whom no church cares. This situation represents hundreds of American communities. Smaller churches, with virile evangelistic impulses, should reach these people for Christ.

I know a church that is composed of a comfortably situated and somewhat proud group of middle class Christians. That church has not grown for twenty-five years though during all of that time it has been evangelistic in appealing to the decent people of its community. The church is situated on the edge of a neighborhood of needy and neglected people. It has never sought to win these spiritually disfranchised persons to Christ. This church really has no prospect of growth unless it is willing to "lose itself" in an effort to win the impoverished.

There is a hazard in seeking to win the religiously disfranchised. Many churches, even evangelical ones, are afraid to try it. They would rather risk their message with the already decent people. With such persons, it seems, a little religious atmosphere will condition them so that they will be acceptable church members. The message might fail, some churches seem to believe, if presented to the alcoholics, the disgraced, and the vile.

Lay visitation evangelism is grass roots evangelism. It is basic to the advance of the church. A pastor in the Middle West says that it took him four years to inspire and train his people in personal witnessing. He states, however, that it was worth every minute he put into it. It is a major Christian achievement in any pastor's life to transform a lethargic church into a crusading evangelistic unit.

Advancing Through Revivals

Revivals have been the outstanding method of Christian advance in America. They are still important and relevant in spite of the fact that a few years ago many churchmen were saying that the days of revivals were over. There is now a resurgence of revival interest that is clearly seen in many local churches and in great city-wide evangelistic campaigns conducted by Billy Graham and other noted evangelists.

In spite of this contemporary resurgence of revival interest, many local churches are conducting revivals that are not great soul winning crusades. Some of these meetings are only short seasons of spiritual refreshment to Christians with little outreach to the world. In such cases the saints are blessed, the faltering are strengthened, and a few backsliders in heart are reclaimed. All of these results are good but they are hardly commensurate with the historical pattern of revivals. It is true that revival meetings must have their origin in the awakening of professing Christians in the church but they must not end there. To paraphrase another, if revivals do not begin in the church, they do not begin, but if they end in the church they *end*.

Revivals are decadent if they do not reach the outside world. The church people should be revived, indeed, but if that is all that happens the revival is little more than a spiritual indulgence. Revival meetings should equip Christians for the winning of souls and the services themselves should become soul winning crusades that reach the lost. Moreover, revivals should continue after the evangelist has gone, as awakened Christians and new converts carry on the work of evangelism through every department of the church.

Revival power is sometimes grounded because of wrong assumptions on the part of churches. Frequently revival meetings are viewed subtly as an easy method of building up the church. In our secular world many people would rather pay a professional soul winner to do the task than to go out and help do it themselves. Moreover, it is often assumed, naively and unconsciously, that an evangelist can bring about a revival. This attitude is frequently fostered by the pastor himself who gives the evangelist a strong build-up in the publicity in an effort to get large congregations. Perhaps the church scheduled the meeting several years in advance and the evangelist crossed the continent to hold the meeting which things suggest that he must be an outstanding person. These things often lead to an overconfidence in the evangelist and accordingly an underconfidence in God and perhaps a lack of thorough spiritual preparation for the meeting. Furthermore, it is sometimes assumed subtly that only revival time is soul winning time. Many people in revivalistic churches do not really expect sinners to be saved in the regular church program. Such an erroneous assumption immobilizes a church in its continued evangelistic efforts. It restricts soul winning.

There is a fine art in arranging for and conducting a revival meeting. Such endeavor demands proper emphases upon prayer, publicity, personal work and preaching. Julian C. McPheeters, out of a long perspective of revival work, both as a pastor and as an evangelist, outlines the following basic revival plans.

I. *Prerevival Steps*

a. Set the date of the revival and secure your preacher several months ahead.

b. Two months before the meetings begin, start cottage meetings in the homes one night during the week, in addition to your regular midweek service.

c. Start your publicity for the meeting with the beginning of the cottage meetings, culminating in an intensified program of publicity two weeks before the meetings start.

d. Enlist all departments of the church in the preparation, having some of your cottage meetings under the auspices of certain departments of the church.

e. Make a survey, and compile a well prepared list of prospects for conversion, for church membership, and for reclamation.

f. Hold a consecration service, and secure volunteers for personal work. Make a well compiled list of the names of the personal workers.

g. Divide your parish into districts, with captains over each district, for carrying on personal work.

h. Turn your midweek service into a class on evangelism for six weeks before the revival begins.

i. Make the last week before the revival begins the most intensive of your preparation. Hold an extra number of cottage meetings this week. Set your goal for an extra large number at the midweek service. Make Friday of this week a 24-hour vigil of prayer. Let the church be open for twenty-four hours beginning at 7 : 00 a.m. and the vigil be kept in half hour periods throughout the day and night by forty-eight people. Let every one be invited to come and spend as much time in the vigil of prayer as possible.

II. *The Revival in Progress*

a. Strike an optimistic vein, and keep it all the way through the meeting.

b. Keep up the publicity and advertising to the last day of the meeting.

c. Observe some special days in the meeting.

d. Organize a telephone brigade, and work it through the captains of the districts.

e. Have special meetings for different groups thirty minutes before the opening of the main service. These groups may be: the young people's group, the women's group, the men's group.

f. Have good music.

g. Have a comfortable house, properly heated and ventilated.

h. Don't hold the service too long.

i. Keep up a systematic campaign of personal evangelism, using the prospects of your survey, and other prospects which the meeting may bring to light.

j. Endeavor to bring the church to Pentecost and the Way of Holiness.

k. Instill into the mind and heart of the church the idea that the special meetings are to prepare the church for an even larger and greater work after the meetings have closed.

III. *Postrevival*

a. Put the new converts to work.

b. Assign all new members to the captains of districts for visitation. Classify your new members, and assign them to the various organizations for enlistment in these organizations.

c. Let the pastor hold a reception in honor of the new members within a week after the close of the special services. Let each new member wear a white tag with name written on it. Introduce the new members, so that the old members may get acquainted with them.

d. Put on a special campaign for attendance at the midweek service.

e. Let every new member be visited by a representative of the official board and secure a voluntary pledge toward the finances of the church.

f. Give special attention to getting all new members present at the first regular communion service after the revival services.

g. Keep up systematic personal evangelism after the meetings are over, enlisting new members in this work also. Keep the converts busy.[8]

Revivalism and lay witnessing complement each other and neither can really be effective without the other. When revivalism ceases in a church the lay witnessing becomes an "evangelism" that is carried on by unrevived persons, a type of ecclesiastical salesmanship designed to get "joiners." When lay witnessing is nonexistent in a church the "evangelism" is a type of ingrown spiritual exercise that does not reach the world. Some authorities estimate that more than ninety per cent of the converts in present-day revivals were first contacted personally by some member of the church.

The smaller church is at its best evangelistically when it lives confidently assured of its own mission and of the power of God. Its evangelistic impulse is strongest when it is sensitive to human needs and unmindful of social classes and distinctions. Its soul winning outreach is greatest when the people are motivated by genuine spiritual concern and go out to witness to the unconverted. Its appeal is widest when it has

---

[8] Julian C. McPheeters, "Revival Plans," *The Christian Minister*, I (October, 1949), pp. 21, 22.

well ordered worship services that have elements of warmth and freedom. Its spiritual power is greatest when it proclaims the eternal gospel that confronts contemporary sins and needs.

It should be noted, as we conclude the pages of this book, that evangelism is the hope of the smaller local church. The larger church with its sizable constituency can carry on its program with less evangelistic emphasis. It can maintain its worship and Christian education programs with a sense of institutional well being without an aggressive evangelistic outlook. The smaller church cannot do this. It must win souls or perish. Some little congregations have lost their evangelistic zeal and they have become extinct. Others are threatened with extinction because of attitudes of discouragement, frustration and defeat.

Evangelism must be the *elan vital,* the vital force, that gives ardor to all of the activities in the little church. This vital force is no supplement added to the program of the church. No official board can vote it in or vote it out. It comes from the very life of the church. It comes as an expression of healthful and vigorous life in the church. It represents a culmination of a strong church program. Thus, in a real sense, all of the emphases of this book are related to evangelism and the growth of the smaller local church.

The growth of any church is a divine-human achievement. It takes both God and man to bring prosperity in the kingdom of God. God gives the increase as people are faithful in prayer, creative in planning, and diligent in service. Such divine-human cooperation brings about the fulfillment of Jesus' words that were spoken to all little Christian groups, "Fear not, little flock; for it is your Father's good pleasure to give you the kingdom" (Luke 12:32).

Appendix

Rating Your Church

"How can you know where you want to go unless you know where you are?" James W. Sells, rural church authority, directs this pointed exhortation to local church leaders. The exhortation is timely. It is as important—and perhaps as difficult—for leaders to know their local churches as organizations as it is for persons to know themselves as individuals. Both groups and individuals are heavily dependent on self-understanding if success is to be achieved.

We are presenting here six rating scales as a practical guide in helping leaders and workers to understand their churches. These scales relate to six basic aspects of church life: organization, stewardship and finance, public relations and publicity, worship, Christian education and evangelism.

Each scale lists some of the important elements and activities that are found in thriving churches. Quite naturally all of the factors are not of equal importance.

The scales may be used by individual persons and by groups and boards as a basis for discussion.

CHURCH ORGANIZATION

Factors To Be Evaluated	Excel.	Good	Avg.	Fair	Poor
Periodic surveys of community needs and opportunities				✓	✓
Clearly envisioned and clearly stated goals					✓
Adequate number of lay workers enlisted					✓
Planned program for training lay workers					✓
Democratic distribution of offices on basis of age, sex, etc.					✓
Sense of mission among lay workers				✓	
Sense of responsibility among lay workers					✓
Church organized to meet needs in its community					✓
Church organized to serve all age groups				✓	
Church organized to provide leadership in worship, Christian education, service, and social activities				✓	
Regular board meetings of church and church school				✓	
Records of all members' abilities, aptitudes and interests available to proper officers					✓
Reports of officers to appropriate committees and boards					✓
Records of the church and all departments carefully kept			✓		
Cooperation with appropriate community agencies					✓
Cooperation with denominational program				✓	

STEWARDSHIP AND FINANCE

Factors To Be Evaluated	Excel.	Good	Avg.	Fair	Poor
Study of financial potential of church			✓		
Emphasis upon stewardship in sermons				✓	
Systematic instruction in stewardship in church school and smaller groups					✓
Tithing maintained as the Christian standard of stewardship			✓		
Annual church budget prepared and accepted by church			✓		
Well-laid plans carried out for stewardship or loyalty Sunday					
Majority of members make annual pledges in loyalty Sunday worship service or in the every member canvass					
Plan for collecting weekly offerings (envelopes or other)			✓		
Offerings received in worship service with dignity and reverence					
Support of denominational program including missions and benevolences				✓	
Proper support of community projects					✓
Long-range plans for providing and maintaining adequate plant and facilities				✓	
Financial records carefully kept			✓		
Financial reports made regularly to members			✓		

Public Relations and Publicity

Factors To Be Evaluated	Excel.	Good	Avg.	Fair	Poor
Church property adequate and well-maintained				✓	
Church services that appeal to un-churched people			✓		
Enthusiasm and morale of members				✓	
Concern for needs of people in community					✓
Welcoming committee and/or ushers greet people that attend worship services	*NEED USHERS AS ESCORTS*				
Working plan of person-to-person publicity					✓
Up-to-date and growing mailing and calling list					✓
Church letters, announcements or parish papers sent once a month to all on mailing list					✓
Church news reported regularly to newspapers					✓
Planned use of paid ads					✓
Planned use of permanent ads: road-side signs and markers, etc.					✓
Outdoor bulletin board carries services, sermon themes and short pithy messages				-	
Church cooperates with other churches in community					✓
Pastor cooperates with public school and public health agencies					
Church encourages community programs for youth: 4H Club, Scouts, recreations, etc.					✓

WORSHIP

Factors To Be Evaluated	Excel.	Good	Avg.	Fair	Poor
Church conducive to worship: clean, well-ventilated, well-heated, hymnals in racks		✓			
Nursery care of small children			✓		
Members punctual at all services					✓
Reverent attitude on part of people on entering sanctuary					✓
Ushers seat people for effective worship					✓
Worshipful congregational singing		✓			
Congregational participation in Scripture readings, responses and music		✓			
Church bulletins used, or announcements made concisely and effectively		✓			
Offering received with dignity and reverence		✓			
Dynamic preaching that appeals to both church members and the unchurched people		✓			
Services frequently brought to a close with persuasive appeal for response		✓			
Both variety and unity in worship services		✓			
Friendliness, yet reverence, following services	✓				

CHRISTIAN EDUCATION

Factors To Be Evaluated	Excel.	Good	Avg.	Fair	Poor
Board of Christian education oversees all religious education activities					✓
Church school recruits capable leaders for all departments, classes and groups					✓
Leadership training by courses, workers' conferences, directed readings, counsel, and assistant teachers and officers					✓
Church carries on adequate Christian education program including weekly Sunday school, young people's organization, children's clubs and Daily Vacation Bible School					✓
Officers and teachers promote attendance					✓
Secretary of absentees and calling committee contact absentees and prospects					✓
General enthusiasm for church school					
Plan for soul winning in church school: evangelistic emphasis in worship and classes, children's evangelistic meetings, personal evangelistic emphasis					✓
Plan for Christian nurture in church school, worship and instruction				✓	
Sunday school promotes church attendance on part of children and youth					
Church school leaders and teachers maintain contact with the homes of the children and youth and with community organizations					✓
Church school organized to provide service opportunities to all members					✓
Records kept faithfully and reports made regularly		✓			

EVANGELISM

Factors To Be Evaluated	Excel.	Good	Avg.	Fair	Poor
Community outreach by helping needy persons					✓
Community outreach by concern for community welfare					✓
Annual community canvass					✓
Organized prayer life: midweek prayer meeting, cottage prayer meetings, pre-revival prayer meetings					✓
Organized group of lay evangelistic visitors					✓
Training for lay evangelistic visitors					✓
Annual week of lay evangelistic visitation					✓
Regular and planned lay evangelistic visitation through year					✓
At least one strong evangelistic service each Sunday					✓
Well-planned annual revival meeting					✓
Well-planned annual youth or children's revival					✓
Support of revival meetings in other nearby churches					✓
Evangelistic church school					✓
Effective plan to train converts for service					✓
Children and youth attend summer camps with evangelistic emphasis					

Index

Achievement, sense of, 50-53
Administration, 88-90
Advertising, 117, 127, 128
Agapes, 21
Apostolic Canons, 93
Apostolic Constitutions, 93
Archibald, Arthur C., 164
Assistants, 75
Atkins, Gaius Glenn, 154
Audio-visual aids, 74

Baptist Training Union, 68
Baptists, 15
Barnette, J. N., 160
Baxter, Richard, 94, 134
Bestimmung, 65
Biblical preaching, 58
Biebe, J. A., 118
Bingham, L. L., 128
Blackwood, Andrew, 88, 121, 126
Bleyer, Willard G., 123
Blizzard, Samuel, 87
Boyd, E. P., 79
Bready, John W., 96
Bruce, A. B., 93
Brunner, Emil, 28
Bryan, Dawson C., 170
Budget, Local Church, 109-113
Buildings, 55, 56, 113-116
Bulletin Boards, 127
Burkhart, Roy A., 18
Buttrick, George A., 18, 41

Cashman, Robert, 118
Chapman, George, 24
Charitable deeds, 100
Chitty, Willard, 109
Choir, 149, 150
Christian nurture, 163-167
Christian service, 21, 27-29, 70,
    77, 166, 167
Church attendance, 10

Church bulletins, 123
Church extension, local, 111
Church merger, 9, 11
Church officers, seniority rights,
    82
Church property, 111
Church, rural, 25, 29
Circuit problems, 84ff
Class meetings, 15, 27
Colby, Frank Moore, 52
Coleman, Robert E., 170
Community canvass, 54, 58-62
Community, status in, 10, 44, 45
Correspondence courses, 75
Corson, Fred, 62
Counseling, 103, 136, 137, 138
Crisis situations, 129, 137
Cults, 99
Curtis, Olin A., 135
Cushman, Ralph, 96, 97

Davis, Warner P., 119
Deacons, 94
DeWitt Memorial Church, 119
Dicks, Russell, 136
Didache, The, 22
Directed readings, 75
Dobbins, Gaines, 109
Douglas, H. P., 46
Douglas, Lloyd, 108

Edwards, Richard Henry, 130
Efficiency, consciousness of, 77
Empathy, 132, 133
Epistle of Barnabas, 22
Eusebius, 104
Evangelical Revival, 14
Evangelism in the Sunday
    School, 160 ff

Fellowship, 21 ff, 165, 166
Finance committee, 56

Finance, desperation, 105
Finance, sub-Christian, 106, 107
Financial potential, 55-57, 105 ff
Francis of Assisi, 14
Franklin, Benjamin, 52, 97
Froebel, F. W. A., 28

Garvie, Alfred E., 155
Glover, T. R., 92
Goals, 62-65
God's Portion Plan, 115
Golay, Eugene A., 170
Gospel, word power, 98
Graham, Billy, 174
Group dynamics, 16, 17
Guiding image, 65

Hall churches, 13
Harnack, Adolf, 103
Harper, E. E., 148, 149
Harral, Stewart, 122
Hebrew Christians, 22
Hollingshead, A. B., 62
Homrighausen, Elmer, 35
Hospitality, spiritual, 36-40
House churches, 13
Hussites, 14

Inferiority feelings, 31
In-service training, 66
Institutional hypochondria, 34
Introvertive churches, 30-41

Jesus, 13, 18, 66, 92, 102, 104,
    108, 140, 166, 169
Job analysis, 69
Judas Maccabeus, 19
Julian the Apostate, 103
Justin, 22

Kaufman, Harold, 62
Kemp, Charles, 134
Kidderminster, 94, 95
Kuist, Howard, 44

Lagemann, John Kord, 132

Lay preaching, 86
Lay visitors, 159
Laymen, enlistment of, 67, 68, 85
Leacock, Stephen, 136
Leadership, 55, 69, 72-76, 89, 90,
    162
Leavell, Roland Q., 87
Lechy, Wm. E. H., 48
Lindsay, Thomas, 13
Liturgical worship, 150 ff
Lobingier, John L., 72, 73
Lollards, 14
Lord's Acre Plan, 115
Love, 133, 134
Lowell, James Russell, 62
Loyalty Sunday, 110, 111-113
Luce, Clayton, 28
Luther, Martin, 104

McPheeters, Julian C., 175
McPherson, Holt, 124
Mailing list, 120-123
Map, plat, 59
Marston, Leslie R., 130
Mayo, Leonard, 88
Methodism, 26
Missions, 111
Money raising organizations,
    professional, 114
Montefiore, C. A., 93
Morale, importance, 43, 44
Moravians, 15
Morley, John, 23
Munger, T. T., 62
Music, church, 147-150

News stories, 124, 125
Newspaper feature articles, 126
Nursery, church, 146

Oates, Wayne, 129
Oberlin, John, 95
Objectives, 62-65
Orchard, W. E., 155
Organization, principles of, 80,
    81

Organization, tasks of, 81-84

Parish paper, 123
Pastor-administrator, 89
Pastoral calling, 58, 136-141
Pastoral letters, 121, 122
Pastoral personality, 130-136
Pastor's salary, 110
Patience, pastoral, 134-136
Patton, Russell R., 78
Paul, 13, 90, 92, 153
Pearce, William, 133
Peary, Robert Edwin, 50
Person-mindedness, 130, 131
Personal participation, 21, 25-27
Personal witnessing, 170
Personality, constructive, 47
Personality, destructive, 47
Pew Plan, 119
Pleuthner, W. A., 120
Preaching, life-situational, 102
Primary groups, 23
Prospect list, 171
Publicity, person-to-person, 11, 80, 120

Quakers, 14, 15

Resources, appraisal of, 53-58
Reverence, 145
Revivals, 166, 174-179
Robb, J. A., 31

Sangster, William, 101
Schaff, Philip, 155
Sells, James W., 182
Sense of belonging, 23, 26
Sherman, Jean K., 101
Singing, congregational, 147-149, 153
Sizoo, Joseph, 119
Smaller church, defined, 9, 10

Smith, H. Augustine, 148
Smith, Rockwell C., 119, 145
Socrates, 55
Southern Baptist Convention, 68
Spiritual assets, 55, 57, 58
Spiritual growth, 25, 107
Status, community, 10, 44, 45
Stewardship, 105-107
Stewardship Sunday, annual, 110
Stuber, Stanley I., 127
Sunday School, 112-113, 157-163
Surveys, community, 59, 60, 69

Telephone Brigades, 119
Tensions, personality, 46-50
Tithing, 109
Trecker, H. B., 63, 88
Troeltsch, Ernst, 33
Trueblood, Elton, 18, 19, 29, 86

Under shepherd plan, 140
Ushers, 39, 146, 147

Visitors, lay, 159

Waldenses, 14
Wayland, Strain, 16
Wedel, Theodore O., 100
Wesley, Charles, 14
Wesley, John, 14, 15, 23, 26, 96, 97
Wesleyan revival, 148
Whitefield, George, 14, 97
Williamson, Glen B., 121, 138
Witnessing, lay, 39, 98-105, 168-174
Workers' library, 75
Worship, 24, 101, 142 ff, 164, 165
Worship, free, 150 ff
Worship, liturgical, 150 ff
Worship, proper conditions for, 143, 144